Ruth Hubbard, Gilles Paquet & Christopher Wilson

Stewardship

Collaborative Decentred Metagovernance
and Inquiring Systems

| Collaborative Decentred Metagovernance Series

This series of books is designed to define cumulatively the contours of collaborative decentred metagovernance. At this time, there is still no canonical version of this paradigm: it is *en émergence*. This series intends to be one of many 'construction sites' to experiment with various dimensions of an effective and practical version of this new approach.

Metagovernance is the art of combining different forms or styles of governance, experimented with in the private, public and volunteer sectors, to ensure effective coordination when power, resources and information are widely distributed, and the governing is of necessity decentred and collaborative.

The series invites conceptual and practical contributions focused on different issue domains, policy fields, *causes célèbres*, functional processes, etc. to the extent that they contribute to sharpening the new apparatus associated with collaborative decentred metagovernance.

In the last few decades, there has been a need felt for a more sophisticated understanding of the governing of the private, public and social sectors: for less compartmentalization among sectors that have much in common; and for new conceptual tools to suggest new relevant questions and new ways to carry out the business of governing, by creatively recombining the tools of governance that have proved successful in all these sectors. These efforts have generated experiments that have been sufficiently rich and wide-ranging in the various laboratories of life to warrant efforts to pull together what we know at this stage.

This first volume in the series attempts to scope out, in a provisional way, the sort of general terrain we are going to explore. It is not meant to impose boundaries or orthodoxies, but only to loosely identify the horizons and the frontiers, as we perceive them at the time of launching this journey. Horizons and frontiers are to us not ways to limit the inquiries, but rather invitations to all forms of transgression.

Interested parties are invited to join the Chautauqua.

– Editorial Board

Titles published by Invenire are listed at the end of the book.

Ruth Hubbard, Gilles Paquet & Christopher Wilson

Stewardship

Collaborative Decentred Metagovernance
and Inquiring Systems

Collaborative Decentred Metagovernance Series
INVENIRE BOOKS

Ottawa, Canada
2012

University of Ottawa **Press**
Les **Presses** de l'Université d'Ottawa

The University of Ottawa Press (UOP) is proud to be the oldest of the francophone university presses in Canada and the oldest bilingual university publisher in North America. Since 1936, UOP has been enriching intellectual and cultural discourse by producing peer-reviewed and award-winning books in the humanities and social sciences, in French and in English.

www.Press.uOttawa.ca

Library and Archives Canada Cataloguing in Publication

Title: Stewardship : collaborative decentred governance and inquiring systems / Ruth Hubbard, Gilles Paquet & Christopher Wilson.
Names: Hubbard, Ruth, 1942- author. | Paquet, Gilles, author. | Wilson, Christopher, 1953- author.
Series: Collaborative decentred metagovernance series.
Description: Series statement: Collaborative decentred metagovernance series | Reprint. Originally published: Ottawa : Invenire Books, 2012. | Includes bibliographical references.
Identifiers: Canadiana (print) 20220286388 | Canadiana (ebook) 2022028640X | ISBN 9780776638614 (softcover) | ISBN 9780776638621 (PDF) | ISBN 9780776638638 (EPUB)
Subjects: LCSH: Public administration—Philosophy. | LCSH: Decentralization in government. | LCSH: Administrative agencies—Philosophy. | LCSH: Social learning. | LCSH: Inquiry-based learning.
Classification: LCC JF1351 .H82 2022 | DDC 351.01/1—dc23

Legal Deposit: Library and Archives Canada, Third Quarter 2022
© University of Ottawa Press 2022, all rights reserved.

This book was initially published by Invenire Books in 2012, in the Collaborative Decentered Metagovernance Series. The initial cover design, layout and design were produced by Sandy Lynch. The University of Ottawa Press reissued this book thanks to the support of Ontario Creates.

Invenire

Invenire Books, an Ottawa-based idea factory that operated from 2010 to 2019, specialized in collaborative governance and stewardship. Invenire and its authors provide creative practical and stimulating responses to the challenges and opportunities faced by today's organizations. The list is now carried by the University of Ottawa Press.

The University of Ottawa Press gratefully acknowledges the support extended to its publishing list by the Government of Canada, the Canada Council for the Arts, the Ontario Arts Council, the Social Sciences and Humanities Research Council and the Canadian Federation for the Humanities and Social Sciences through the Awards to Scholarly Publications Program, and by the University of Ottawa.

ONTARIO ARTS COUNCIL
CONSEIL DES ARTS DE L'ONTARIO
an Ontario government agency
un organisme du gouvernement de l'Ontario

Canada Council   Conseil des arts
for the Arts   du Canada

Canada

uOttawa

"In theory, there's no difference between theory and practice. In practice, there is."

– *Yogi Berra*

Table of Contents

| Introduction

"Governments are no longer in charge."   "Nobody in charge..."
                               – *John Gray*   – *Harlan Cleveland*

This short book is a simultaneous call for modesty, pragmatism and optimism. Modesty is a result of the growing recognition that we live in a society of complex adaptive systems characterized by "a large number of interacting and interdependent elements in which there is no central control; self-organizing and emergent behaviours based on sophisticated information-processing generate learning, evolution and development ... (an environment) in which what to do to solve problems is uncertain and key stakeholders are in conflict about how to proceed."[1] In such contexts, governing is a most daunting task: pragmatically, it cannot be done without the collaboration of key stakeholders (who have part of the information, resources and power) and the consent of the governed.

In our experience, there has been a reluctance to confront this daunting task, and a propensity to invoke simplifying assumptions in order to make the task look more tractable. For instance, many have fallen into the bad habits of assuming (1) that someone is always in charge in organizations and social systems (i.e., someone who has all the information, the power and the resources required to steer the system in preferred directions), and (2) that this 'leader' has a way to divine

---

[1] Michael Quinn Patton. 2011. *Developmental Evaluation – Applying Complexity Concepts to Enhance Innovation and Use*. New York: The Guilford Press, p. 1.

these preferred directions from the expert knowledge of the members' shared values. This caricature-like, simplified version of the governing scene we have labeled Big 'G' (government) – stereotypically associated with government, although it is present in the private and social sectors as well – and it has generated copious literature on the subject of 'leadership', widely available at the local airport.

These sorts of simplifications have proven to be grossly deceptive. Experience has shown that, except in the most trivial situations, no one has all the information, the power and the resources required to steer any social system effectively (i.e., nobody is really fully in charge),[2] and that, in a pluralist world, where members have different values and identities, shared values are a myth.[3] In this situation, the best governance outcome one can expect to achieve is an agreement by heterogeneous members, for all sorts of quite different reasons, on a set of principles, norms or rules of *vivre-ensemble* likely to help nudge the organization or the social system toward some form of effective coordination. This is what we have labeled small 'g' (governance), and it has generated its own growing literature that argues for the replacement of the notion of leadership with that of stewardship.[4]

In a practical way, the complex and turbulent context in which modern governing is pursued is continually evolving in uncertain and unpredictable ways, such that practitioners in the private, public, and social sectors have been frustrated by the failures of Big 'G' apparatuses (top down and authoritarian) to ensure effective coordination among the various stakeholders. Pragmatically, they have been led to search for new tools, discovering *en route* the notion of effective stewardship – at once bottom-up, based on partnership, collaboration and experimentation, and the capacity of combining all sorts of mechanisms that tap into the knowledge and information

[2] Harlan Cleveland. 2002. *Nobody in Charge*. San Francisco: Jossey-Bass.

[3] Joseph Heath. 2003. *The Myth of Shared Values in Canada*. Ottawa: Canadian Centre for Management Development.

[4] Peter Block. 1993. *Stewardship*. San Francisco: Berrett-Koehler.

held by key stakeholders, that is, the requisite knowledge and information to construct an effective governance apparatus.

This attempt to replace romanticized and personalized leadership by collaborative stewardship (i.e., by an ensemble of mechanisms ensuring effective coordination and innovation when power, resources and information are distributed among many, and when there are no shared values acting as a North Star to guide this process) has prompted our metagovernance work – efforts to combine, blend, or compound different forms or styles of governing instruments that have been separately experimented with in the private, public and social sectors in order to ensure effective stewardship in particular issue domains.

What is collaborative decentred metagovernance?

In more recent times, the label 'metagovernance' has been hijacked by unrepentant public sector Big-'G'-ers to connote the supposedly necessary supervisory role of state control in new forms of mixed governance in order to 'rescue' the traditional top-down cosmology, both in the small – within the public sector – and in the large – where it is presumed that the state is the only legitimate principal actor empowered to impose top-down on society, a "hierarchical governance that coordinates network and market styles of governance."[5] But this is a futile salvaging operation: the state is neither in charge of all things nor need it always be the grand coordinator *en dernière instance* (in the small or in the large) in the governing of a complex adaptive system. Governing is co-produced at both levels by the interactions among many key stakeholders and their rapport with the context.

'Collaborative decentred metagovernance' is therefore fundamentally heterarchical: demanding that the stakeholders share commitment and control, but, within this collaborative context, the mechanisms of integration of hierarchies, markets and networks may each dominate in turn or concurrently in

---

[5] Louis Meuleman. 2008. *Public Management and the Metagovernance of Hierarchies, Networks and Markets*. Heidelberg: Physic-Verlag, p. 72.

the emergent, composite governance patterns depending on need. Collaborative decentred metagovernance thus connotes the ways in which the different families of mechanisms (or particular blends or mixes of them) get 'orchestrated'[6] by different stakeholders, in different ways, according to the circumstances.[7] This is the sense in which the term 'collaborative decentred metagovernance' is used here.

For Bevir and Rhodes, this approach is the result of a third wave of reactions to the failures of Big 'G' government – after the first wave of new public management and its greater use of markets and quasi-markets, and the second wave of metagovernance, where the state attempted to impose obliquely its quarterbacking by pretending to be the only one to be allowed to metagovern. This third wave announces a *de facto* collaborative decentred metagovernance that recognizes that multiple stakeholders will create a contingent pattern of rules through their diverse understandings and conflicting actions. For Bevir and Rhodes, this announces the arrival of the stateless state: the contingent product of the diverse actions, practices and struggles informed by the beliefs of the stakeholders.[8]

The best way to map the collaborative decentred metagovernance terrain and to define a platform for this budding *problematique* is to build on an adaptation of the graphical apparatus used by Kenneth Boulding (Figure 1).

The Boulding triangle represents the various combinations of the forces of coercion (hierarchy), exchange (market) and solidarity (network) that might be blended in an effort to distill the sort of mixed arrangements capable of providing effective coordination when power, resources

---

[6] It being understood that the orchestra is conductorless … see Harvey Seifter and Peter Economy. 2002. *Leadership Ensemble – Lessons in Collaborative Management from the World-Famous Conductorless Orchestra*. New York: Times Books.

[7] Gerard Fairtlough. 2005. *The Three Ways of Getting Things Done*. Dorset UK: The Triarchy Press.

[8] Mark Bevir and R.A.W. Rhodes. 2010. *The State as Cultural Practice*. Oxford: Oxford University Press, chapter 5.

and information are widely distributed.[9] The virtue of this distillation comes by tapping into the varieties of knowledge available to the various stakeholders, and taking full advantage of the dynamics of the context.[10]

FIGURE 1. The Adapted Boulding Triangle

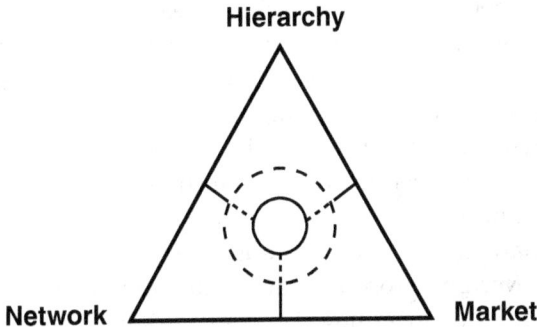

Hierarchy

Network   **Market**

To respond better to the increasingly complex, plural, and fragmented nature of the organizations and social systems and of their contexts, the governing apparatus must make a fuller and better use of the wide array of integrating and coordination mechanisms that are already available and have been experimented with in the diverse sectors. Taken together, these collaborative arrangements are bound to be diversified, plural and pluralist, and their collective patterns depend on both the dynamics of the environment and the creative designs of contributing social architects. These mixes of mechanisms are 'located' at the center of Figure 1.

[9] Eva Sorensen and Jacob Torfing (eds.). 2007. *Theories of Democratic Network Governance*. London: Palgrave Macmillan.

[10] This approach to the organizational terrain being a mix of hierarchy, market and networks as mechanisms of coordination originated with Kenneth E. Boulding (*A Primer on Social Dynamics*. New York: The Free Press, 1970) and was used extensively in our approach to collaborative governance over the last decade (Gilles Paquet. 1999. *Governance Through Social Learning*. Ottawa: University of Ottawa Press). A cognate graphical apparatus has resurfaced under the label of metagovernance more recently (Louis Meuleman. 2008. *Public Management and the Metagovernance of Hierarchies, Networks and Markets*. Heidelberg: Physic-Verlag).

This approach not only challenges the hollowness of the notion of leadership, but also shakes off the dominance of disciplines (political studies in public administration, economics in private management, and sociology in civic or social organizations), and suggests the need for a more comprehensive, composite and multidisciplinary language of problem definition to match the increasingly complex and turbulent nature of both the environment and the governance process. It emphasizes the need to reframe our perspectives if we want to be effective in reconfiguring the value space.[11]

This new *manière de voir* entails a major challenge of the assumptions on which the traditional conceptual apparatus is built, and a major transformation in the nature of the relevant units of analysis, in the sort of skills required in practice to co-produce governing processes, and in the overall nature of the very ambitions of governing. This new paradigm is not meant to displace the earlier ones, but rather to integrate them into a broader, more encompassing, and heuristically more powerful approach. It has the added advantage of throwing some useful critical light on the limitations of simplistic arrangements masquerading as superior forms or styles of governance or as panaceas.

A work in progress

The collaborative decentred metagovernance approach is a work in progress, and, consequently, this book and this series are of necessity open-ended.

This first volume in the Collaborative Decentred Metagovernance series is meant neither to propose a comprehensive survey of the state of the art, nor to present any sort of orthodox point of view. Attempting to cover the waterfront of the literature on the emerging collaborative decentred metagovernance in a small introductory book would be impossible. As for propounding an orthodox view to which all would be invited to adhere, that would be a most unhelpful

[11] Richard Normann. 2001. *Reframing Business – When the Map Changes the Landscape*. New York: Wiley & Sons.

way to introduce what attempts to be a multiplex approach to the protean texture of collaborative decentred metagovernance.

Yet if this starting point is to be useful in providing the series with a foundation of some sort, it must at the very least identify certain families of issues that the new collaborative decentred metagovernance approach needs to address if it is to provide practical insights into new lines of questioning, new units of analysis, new organizational architecture, and new relational skills that may be capable of taking advantage of any heuristically enhanced approach. That is, if collaborative decentred metagovernance is to be useful, then it must, at a minimum, improve the bottom-up capacity to tweak and repair defective governance arrangements, or invent more promising ones – what we refer to, somewhat light-heartedly, as 'scheming virtuously'.[12]

The focal point of this first volume in the series is therefore the notion of 'stewardship' and the challenges of constructing governance conversations as a way to generate a sort of 'super automatic pilot' (if we may be permitted to use this metaphor) by tapping into the varied existing knowledge, and by combining a variety of mechanisms so that the organization or social system can be not only resilient, but have the capacity to transform and innovate in the face of a continuously evolving context.

In this volume, we have chosen to focus on five sets of issues that might be regarded as core building blocks of stewardship in the collaborative decentred metagovernance approach.

The imperfect prototype we put forward is meant only to initiate a conversation: its components are contestable, and should be contested. But, whatever the alternative perspectives on these issues might be, it is our view that any practitioner of collaborative decentred metagovernance will have to take a stand on how to deal with these issues, if one is to dramatically reframe the way in which problems are defined, to refurbish the design process of metagovernance, and to conceptualize the emerging notion of stewardship that is anchored in the mix of

---

[12] Gilles Paquet. 2009. *Scheming virtuously: the road to collaborative governance.* Ottawa: Invenire Books.

coordinating mechanisms that can be drawn from the whole ensemble of mechanisms described by the Boulding triangle.[13] Moreover, it will be possible on the basis of this prototype to critically redefine in a much more sophisticated way how public policy must be redefined (from a focus on goal-and-control to one on intelligence and innovation) for effective intervention in the world of complex adaptive systems.

A preview of the contents

Five clusters of questions are dealt with in the following chapters.

Chapter 1 has an 'epistemological' flavour. It asks what are the new paradigms and attendant metaphors that are needed to make sense of this more distributed governance reality. It tries to partially map some of the knowledge base underpinning the collaborative decentred metagovernance approach: first and foremost, it underlines the sort of quantum perspective that is needed to replace the Newtonian cosmology in good currency in policy sciences; but it also identifies the basic assumptions, the key concepts, the stewardship dynamics, and the process of 'collibration' (tipping the balance, nudging the balance to compensate) that are the required building blocks for a stewardship built on inquiring systems.

Chapter 2 puts front and centre a 'social learning' perspective as the most promising lens through which one can define stewardship through collaborative decentred metagovernance. It asks why social learning is so central to collaborative decentred metagovernance and how it can be fostered. This requires a shift from Big 'G' (government) – hierarchical, centralized, authoritarian, coercive – to small 'g' (governance) – pluralist, participative, experimentalist – in all sectors (private, public and social). We make the case for governance as 'inquiring systems', as assemblages of learning heuristics. We then venture a provisional checklist of questions that might help in guiding the production of an effective regime

[13] Gilles Paquet. 2009. "Stewardship versus Leadership" in *Scheming virtuously: the road to collaborative governance*, chapter 5.

of collaborative decentred metagovernance. Such checklists will be most useful as affordances or ways to take advantage of past experiences in the various contexts where stewardship needs to emerge,[14] and where collaboration shapes stewardship.

Chapter 3 focuses on the way the collaboration imperative that underpins stewardship materializes through 'scheming virtuously'. It asks how leadership-dominated organizations can be transformed into stewardship-based organizations with shared ownership. It reports on the ways in which the collaborative decentred metagovernance of self-regulating networks, hierarchies and markets unfolds as an inquiring system, and on the crystallization of the outcomes of such collaborative activities in keeping with the dual imperative of effective social learning – that is, to produce the requisite balance of resilience and capacity to transform, and the obligation for collaborative decentred metagovernance to ensure that the organization navigates within an acceptable ethical corridor – while being fully conscious that this steering may fail on both fronts.

Chapter 4 asks how the focus on stewardship can reframe the way in which the public policy process is conceived. It examines the different phases of social learning as 'emerging wayfinding', emphasizes the centrality of fail-safe and safe-fail mechanisms in a process that is always likely to fail because of the complexity of the context, and illustrates why and how such failures occur, and how effective stewardship might help to generate the needed repairs in two issue domains – healthcare policy, and productivity and innovation policy.

Chapter 5 probes a much thornier set of problems that emerge when organizations or social systems face a need to reinvent themselves because of 'changes of kind' either in the context or in the appreciative system. It asks how collaborative decentred metagovernance can respond to discontinuities or fundamental changes. It is then no longer sufficient for stewardship to rely on tinkering with strategies or policies.

[14] Atul Gawande. 2009. *The Checklist Manifesto – How to Get Things Right*. New York: Metropolitan Books.

There is a need to creatively respond by reframing the issues, and for stewardship to ensure that the 'collaborative decentred metagovernance styles' are subjected to a fundamental governance review. Two case studies (mental health, and the interfaces with some Aboriginals) illustrate the sort of challenges faced in such moments of 'creative destruction', and hint at the fact that the very notion of rationality in use has to be transformed in such situations if there is to be any possibility of overcoming these difficulties.

The conclusion tallies some lessons learned, reflects on the various avenues that this new collaborative decentred metagovernance platform would appear to open, and argues that stewardship requires developmental evaluation.

Envoi

This first volume in the series has two main purposes: to define the ambit of what we call inquiring systems, collaborative decentred metagovernance and stewardship broadly, and to illustrate how the new cosmology suggests alternative forms of inquiry.

The template used in this first volume of the series is not meant to apply to the following volumes in a rigid way. As suggested in the presentation of the series, the intent is for each volume to contribute to identifying, in a particular and somewhat idiosyncratic way, some of the contours of stewardship and collaborative decentred metagovernance, and to help in rethinking the possibilities opened by the new cosmology.

Each book in the series may be read separately, but it is our hope that each separate volume will be helpful in shaping a better collaborative decentred metagovernance approach, and therefore better stewardship. Improving the inquiry and the emerging wayfinding processes will be the guiding philosophy of the series: there is no assured pathway in this sort of exploration and prospection, but much discovery and social learning.

CHAPTER 1

| Foundations

Gilles Paquet

"You are not thinking, you are just being logical."
– *Niels Bohr*

Thinking about collaborative decentred metagovernance and stewardship entails the changing of certain habits of mind that have had a very bad influence on the discussions about governing. While the ensemble of new perspectives connoted by collaborative decentred metagovernance has not yet been pulled together into a full-fledged and well-structured cosmology, observers have acknowledged that the features of this budding *problematique* stand in sharp contrast with those associated with the traditional cosmology, and that the emergence of a new mindset requires the recognition of the central importance of certain particularly new assumptions, concepts and forces at work.

A new mindset

The traditional cosmology in good currency in social sciences has a Newtonian flavour: the world is presented as a set of mechanical and predictable objects, as a whole that is no more than the sum of its parts, capable of being broken down into component parts that can be studied piecemeal, and can be "understood through rational inquiry based on objectivity, certainty and chain reasoning ... It is based on certainty, order, structure, status and determinism."[15]

The corollaries of these Newtonian assumptions are well-known and widely accepted by conventional social scientists: individualism (humans as separate and self-contained); hedonistic psychology (motivations are precise, rational and predictable); equality (each human being is commensurable and interchangeable); mutual exclusivity (humans cannot occupy the same place at the same time without conflict and power relations ensuing), and each human pursues his own self-interest in this individualistic dog-eat-dog world.[16] Moreover, it is presumed that, through some not-always-well-understood processes, leaders can distil the 'aggregate preferences' of their deferent or fearful followers, and rationally guide the organization or the social system keeping within these guideposts.

These assumptions are highly contestable: humans are most often best defined by their environment and relationships, rather than by their innate preferences; their desires, intentions, and talents are unequal; they share space and collaborate; their behaviour is not determined only by external stimuli, but also by discourse, deliberation, and herd movements; and the individual-ranked preferences cannot be aggregated into a consistent community-wide ranking.[17]

The Newtonian world is too simplistic, too absolute and too limited to be able to provide a useful representation of our complex and turbulent world. The pretence, for instance, that through elite accommodation or other contraptions, the state can elicit transcendent, commonly agreed-upon values that would serve as guideposts is pure fantasy. This has greatly

[15] Christa Daryl Slaton. 1991. "Quantum Theory and Political Theory" in Theodore L. Becker, (ed). *Quantum Politics – Applying Quantum Theory to Political Phenomena*. New York: Praeger, p. 42-43.

[16] Christa Daryl Slaton, 1991, p. 45-47; Benjamin Barber. 1984. *Strong Democracy*. Berkeley: University of California Press.

[17] Christa Daryl Slaton, 1991, p. 48; Benjamin Barber, 1984, p. 42.

crippled the traditional approaches to governing organizations and social systems, to the point where some have referred to traditional political science as an "antiquarian discipline,"[18] and indicted the social sciences as seemingly trapped in a stage of development that is not unlike the state of biology when it classified animals according to the number of legs.

The idea that anyone can know reality in all its details is a fiction. Traditional and mechanical notions of rationality and cause-effect determinism are also unduly simplistic. The chasms between such simplified representations and the full richness of experience is increasingly bound to force social sciences (and political science, in particular) to abandon the old cosmology, and to adopt a more sensible set of representations based on a sort of quantum perspective.

In the quantum world, the major principles are quite different:
- objects are defined by their environments and their relationships with others;
- cause-effect determinism and rational decision making are not at the root of all human interactions;
- human systems are dynamic, moving processes that most often cannot be divided into discrete units for analysis; and
- there is no objective, real world apart from one's consciousness.

The quantum perspective recognizes that human beings are unpredictable and contradictory in nature, that it is often impossible to determine cause and effect except in probabilistic terms, and that in the process of social learning and collaboration which underpin human activities much is to be ascribed to beliefs and emotions. It entails a redefinition of rationality as ecological fit, and of the policy process as inquiring and 'wayfinding' systems – freed from the naïveties of assuming that rationality is simple internal coherence, and of the caricatures of the policy/strategy process as goal-control and bow-arrow-target contraptions, as suggested by the traditional paradigm.

[18] Glendon A. Schubert. 1983. "The Evolution of Political Science: Paradigms of Physics, Biology and Politics," *Politics and the Life Sciences* (1): 98.

Obviously, this calls for revisiting many assumptions in good currency, for modifying the vocabulary used to define the problems, for adding key concepts to the intellectual tool box, and for reconceiving the whole dynamic of stewardship of human systems on the basis of fundamental uncertainty, limited information, experimentation, social learning, continuous interactions that modify the very settings of the game. Moreover, the broader megacommunity, the powerful impact of the environment, and the forces of self-organization must be taken seriously as forces of co-governance.

John G. Heilman has provided a most interesting survey of past and living social scientists who were quite conscious of those challenges, and has shown (as illustration) how the institutional analysis of Elinor Ostrom (a recent Nobel prize winner in economics) is based on a conceptual framework that has factored in comprehensiveness, recursiveness and creativity by adopting a quantum perspective in her research.[19] One might say the same thing about the work of Charles Sabel.[20]

Not all participants in the conversations about stewardship, collaborative decentred metagovernance, and inquiring systems agree on all aspects of this dramatic paradigm shift, on the central importance of the same particular assumptions or of the same key concepts as mental tools. Nor do they hold the same view about the nexus of forces shaping the stewardship of organizations and social systems, and thus about the most effective ways to nudge organizations and social systems in desirable directions. But the material surveyed below may be regarded as a somewhat representative assemblage of the

[19] John G. Heilman. 1991. "Present at the Creation: A Quantum Perspective on the Methodology of Political Research" in Theodore L. Becker, (ed). *Quantum Politics – Applying Quantum Theory to Political Phenomena.* New York: Praeger, p. 201-219; Elinor Ostrom. 2005. *Understanding Institutional Diversity.* Princeton, NJ: Princeton University Press.

[20] Charles F. Sabel. 2001. "A Quiet Revolution of Democratic Governance : Towards Democratic Experimentalism" in Wolfgang Michalski et al. *Governance in the 21st Century.* Paris: OECD, p. 121-148.

sort of changes in the mindset and in the *outillage mental* that will have to accompany the shift from views associated with the traditional Newtonian cosmology to the quantum views aligned with collaborative decentred metagovernance.

Assumptions

The new mindset is built on three important assumptions: the primacy of process; the centrality of design; and the fact that reflexivity is consubstantial with any effective stewardship.

These three assumptions of the new mindset are ways to respond to three weaknesses of the old mindset plagued by its assumptions about a mechanical object-world; its view of decision making and problem solving as occurring within a maze-like world where the problem is purported to be already set; and a neglect of human intentionality and belief systems in governance processes.

Process

The process approach does not deny that things or objects exist, but it suggests that stable structures are rooted in the processes that have generated them, and are best understood through an analysis of these processes that remains unfinished and open-ended.

The process approach and the object approach are traditions that have their roots in classical Greece, in the opposition of Heraclitus and Parmenides, and the lineage of each tradition is impressive. But the object tradition has been overwhelmingly dominant in the social sciences of the 20th century as a result of the impact of positivism. Emile Durkheim, maybe more than anyone else, has been associated with the doctrine that *"les faits sociaux sont des choses,"* and should be approached as such. Friedrich Hayek has torpedoed positivism and scientism as unfit for the social sciences, and Jules Monnerot wrote a most celebrated denunciation of Durkheim's stance, but these attacks did not have a determinant impact: most mainstream social sciences have remained associated with positivism and the object approach, and human agency has played second fiddle.[21]

There has been a recent shift to a focus on process, emphasizing a dynamic open-ended approach in terms of flows.[22] It has aptly restated the basic tenets of process philosophy, and anti-reductionist social scientists have begun to see the human world as consisting of processes.

Design

An offshoot of the process perspective is that intervening in the process is in the nature of design. But design cannot be reduced to problem-solving steps, fully programmable under a set of rules.[23] This is unduly reductive, since it assumes that the problem space (like an actual maze) has a structure that is already given.

The design process does not really start with such givens. Schön defines it as intelligent exploration of a terrain (p. 125), as an inquiry guided by an appreciative system carried over from history and past experience that produces "a selective representation of an unfamiliar situation that sets values for the system's transformation. It frames the problem of the problematic situation and thereby sets directions in which solutions lie and provides a schema for exploring them" (p. 131-132).

Designing is a conversation with the situation that leads to experimenting with rules, and guideposts that, in turn, reveal conflicts and dilemmas in the appreciative system. Since participants talk across discrepant frames, designing "is a process in which communication, political struggle, and substantive inquiry are combined ... [and it] may be judged appropriate ... if it leads to the creation of a design structure

---

[21] Emile Durkheim. (1894) 1973. *Les règles de la méthode sociologique*. Paris: Presses Universitaires de France; Friedrich A. Hayek. 1952. *Scientism and the Science of Society*. Glencoe, IL: The Free Press; Jules Monnerot. 1946. *Les faits sociaux ne sont pas des choses*. Paris: Gallimard.

[22] Nicholas Rescher. 2000. *Process Philosophy*. Pittsburg: University of Pittsburg Press.

[23] Donald A. Schön. 1990. "The Design Process" in V.A. Howard, (ed.). *Varieties of Thinking*. New York: Routledge, p. 110-141.

that directs inquiry toward progressively greater inclusion of features of the problematic situation and values for its transformation" (p. 138-139). Such exploration leads to learning by doing, and "involves inquiry into systems that do not yet exist."[24] This new way of thinking builds on experimentation, prototyping and serious play,[25] and makes the highest and best use of grappling, grasping, discerning, and sense-making as part of reflective generative learning.[26]

Reflexivity

Reflexivity is defined by Bob Jessop as "the ability and commitment to uncover and make explicit to oneself the nature of one's intentions, projects and actions and their conditions of possibility; and, in this context, to learn about them, critique them, and act upon any lessons that have been learnt."[27]

Reflexivity means that knowledge acquired gets integrated during the inquiry, and unfolds in order to modify the outcome.

Traditional social sciences have done a very poor job of factoring in the human capacity for representational re-description. The belief systems underpinning these representations have an immense impact on the institutions themselves. The new mindset recognizes that the complexity and turbulence of the context is such that agents cannot fully

---

[24] A.G.L. Romme. 2003. "Making a Difference: Organization as Design," *Organization Science*, 14 (5): 558.

[25] Prototyping means (1) identifying as quickly as possible some top requirements, (2) putting in place a quick-and-dirty provisional medium of co-development, (3) allowing as many interested parties as possible to get involved as partners in designing a better arrangement, (4) encouraging iterative prototyping, and (5) thereby encouraging all, through playing with prototypes, to get a better understanding of the problems, of their priorities and of themselves (Gilles Paquet. 2009. *Crippling Epistemologies and Governance Failures – A Plea for Experimentalism*. Ottawa: University of Ottawa Press, p. 8; Michael Schrage. 2000. *Serious Play*. Boston: Harvard Business School Press, p. 199ff).

[26] R.P. Chait et al. 2005. *Governance as Leadership*. Hoboken, NJ: Wiley, chapter 6.

[27] Bob Jessop. 2003. *Governance and Metagovernance: On Reflexivity, Requisite Variety, and Requisite Irony*, p. 7, http://comp.lancs.uk/sociology/soc108rj.htm.

understand and grasp it. This entails a process of inquiry with a built-in, ongoing critical ability to think about the implications of particular choices, and an ongoing capacity to modify means and ends as learning evolves. It means learning how to learn reflexively.

Key concepts

Three important sets of concepts flow from the worldview or cosmology on which the new paradigm is built: the centrality of the notions of information and knowledge, of networks, and of interactions and collaboration in understanding the ways in which effective coordination is effected when power, resources and information are widely distributed – which is the definition of governance.

Information and knowledge

Rather than defining organizations as a set of roles and rules ossified in an organizational chart, the new collaborative decentred metagovernance probes organizations by defining their 'informational' DNA – that is, the nature of the messages exchanged, and the contribution of the organizational capital in producing knowledge and competencies.

The type of messages exchanged defines the texture of the organization: primarily anonymous signals in a free market, commands in a hierarchy, empathetic communication in solidarity associations, mixed messages in hybrid organizations, etc.

Organizations contribute to social learning and to the increase of knowledge and competencies by making good use of the available information and knowledge. Indeed, this is the core task of design: to modify the informational texture of organizations in such a way as to transform the incentives and motivations, and thus accelerate the process of learning since it is the source of value-adding and innovation.

Networks

Networks are ways of organizing the production of information, knowledge and collaboration. They constitute the hard core of organizational and cognitive capital and embody the capacity to create some articulation between technical learning and relational learning. They may take many forms, but are rooted in some voluntary participation. They entail strong 'responsibilization' and are important drivers not only of learning, but also of the construction of identities.[28]

The notion of network is quite protean and may apply equally well to small and mass phenomena: it is a very effective means of building relationships that economizes the costs of transacting, and makes collaboration easier. It may also throw much light on the blockages that can transform fluid networks into gridlock, making collaboration difficult and even impossible.[29]

Collaboration

Collaboration is what breathes life into a network. It may take many forms and deploy itself in creative waves as well as in destructive tsunamis. The core challenge in collaborative metagovernance is to understand how collaboration emerges and persists. One must understand the necessary conditions that would ensure that, from these interactions, will emerge the habits and conventions that will produce relatively stable and regular connections, and the capacities to adjust and adapt to the actions of others in a manner that generates social learning, smooth transformations, and creative ways to resolve crisis situations in the organization.

Collaborative decentred metagovernance starts from the basic premise that nobody is in charge, and that only collaboration can generate effective coordination in a world where power, resources, and information are widely distributed.

---

[28] Yochai Benkler. 2006. *The World of Networks: How Social Production Transforms Markets and Freedom*. New Haven: Yale University Press.

[29] Michael Heller. 2008. *The Gridlock Economy – How Too Much Ownership Wrecks Markets, Stops Innovation, and Costs Lives*. New York: Basic Books.

Collaboration is dependent upon communication generating social negotiation and creative output. Such collaboration has been observed and studied in animal societies, where it has been shown that explicit and conscious social negotiation was *not* necessary for collaboration to materialize. It is in this context that Pierre-Paul Grasse coined the term 'stigmergy' to connote a method of communication (and implicit negotiation) in which individuals communicate with one another by modifying their local environment. It helps us to understand "how disparate, distributed, *ad hoc* contributions could lead to the emergence of the largest collaborative enterprises."[30]

A new trans-disciplinary approach has developed to provide the new literacy needed to understand and make sense of collaboration. Its origin is in the emergence of social dilemmas in which individual rationality would appear to lead to collective irrationality. The best example is the tragedy of the commons, where common property resources are depleted by the overuse of the resource as the result of each myopic individual trying to make the highest and best use of it for him/herself.

A relatively simple and yet powerful avenue out of this sort of dilemma is the development of a broader perspective through generating common knowledge: partaking in rituals producing common knowledge, that is, letting all know exactly what other audience members know. Once, other persons' views are made known, collaboration is made possible. Indeed, increasing common knowledge becomes a way to foster coordination and collaboration.[31]

This has been illustrated vividly by simulations of fishing banks games – a simplified world of commercial fishing without foreign competition and corrupt or incompetent regulators, just people trying to grow their fishing business. Each company begins with a number of boats, a bank account and a set of options to choose from (deep water, shallow water

[30] M. Elliott. 2006. "Stigmergic Collaboration: The Evolution of Group Work," *M/C Journal*, 9(2). http:ééjournal.media-culture.org.aué0605é03-elliott.php [retrieved March 7, 2012].

[31] M.S.W. Chwe. 2001. *Rational Ritual*. Princeton, NJ: Princeton University Press.

fishing, etc.) and information on each fishery, like how rapidly fish stock regenerate. The simulation game usually covers a 10-year period.

For decades, the game has been played by various groups from the public, private and social sectors and, in almost every case, it has resulted in overfishing and the collapse of the fishery. But collapse is not inevitable. In a workshop hosted by Harley-Davidson, the Harley team refused to go ahead with the game until every team agreed to share information about fish catches – reasoning that this information was necessary to monitor overall supply. The Harley team (having avoided a near extinction of their company in the 1980s by a mix of competition and collaboration) also elected to announce to each other, each year, whether or not they were going to expand their fleet (even though such disclosure was not required). This prompted others to do the same. The result was that the fishery never collapsed. The industry regulated itself. Profits and total assets of all teams were higher than for any other game.[32]

Saveri et al. have provided a synthesis of the recent work on collaboration, not in simulations, but in practical experiences, and shown that concepts of synchrony, symbiosis, group selection, catalysis, commons, collective action and collective intelligence provide the raw material from which one may draw a description of the dynamics that can be fine tuned to foster cooperation. Building on this platform, Saveri et al. have suggested a strategic map of cooperation-amplifying technologies, and suggested ways to leverage these technologies of collaboration.[33]

The usefulness of these technologies has been illustrated by reference to a wide variety of successful experiences in the private, public and social sectors. The work of Charles Sabel

[32] Peter Senge et al. 2010. *The Necessary Revolution.* New York: Broadway Books, p. 170-172; for additional information about the corporate culture built on continual talk across boundaries at Harley-Davidson, see Rich Teerlink and L. Osley. 2000. *More than a Motorcycle.* Cambridge, MA: Harvard Business School.

[33] A. Saveri et al. 2004. *Toward a New Literacy of Cooperation in Business.* Menlo Park: Institute for the Future; A. Saveri et al. 2005. *Technologies of Cooperation.* Menlo Park: Institute for the Future.

has shown how the public policy process can be informed and improved using those technologies.[34]

Stewardship as process

The prime mover in stewardship is a capacity for the organization to learn, that is, to reflect on its own experience, to make sense of it, and to retool, restructure, and even to reframe the basic questions facing the organization in order to generate effective ways to discern and grapple with the generative challenge of learning. Social learning crystallizes in a collective intelligence that effectively mobilizes some of the existing knowledge and competencies (emerging from self-organization or design) as one would observe it – in a daring metaphor – in a kind of super automatic pilot.[35]

There is a fundamental difference between 'leadership' (a notion so central to the old cosmology and, traditionally, supposedly embodied in a person of exceptional quality capable of guiding the organization or social system top-down), and 'stewardship' (the central notion in the new cosmology, defined as a 'wayfinding' capacity emerging from social learning and embodied in a mix of mechanisms – some designed but some organic – generating coordination, resilience, innovation, overcoming and accomplishment). Leadership is anchored in the notion of hierarchy, while stewardship is anchored in a mix of mechanisms and styles of governance, inspired by a blend of hierarchy, market and network solidarity forces.

A particular mix of mechanisms may work well until the organization faces major unforeseen disturbances, at which time disaster forces some tinkering with the automatic pilot. This is routinely done after an air travel disaster, when the aircraft has faced heretofore unmet weather circumstances with which the automatic pilot was unable to cope. As a result, it is improved to be able to cope with such circumstances next time.

[34] Charles F. Sabel. 2001. "A Quiet Revolution of Democratic Governance...," p. 121-148.

[35] Gilles Paquet. 2009. *Scheming virtuously: the road to collaborative governance.* Ottawa: Invenire Books, chapter 5.

Such overhauling triggered by experience ensures, more or less, that the requirements for effective stewardship are in place. These requirements have been spelled out by practitioners of reflexive governance: knowledge integration and learning by doing; sensitivity to long-run anticipation of systemic effects; adaptivity of strategies and institutions; iterative experimental and participatory definition of broad directions; and interactive strategy development.[36]

Stewardship is embodied both in competencies and capacities, and in certain dynamics emanating from the milieu.

Competencies/capabilities

These required competencies may be divided into five categories:
1. contextual: embracing uncertainty and error, building bridges, reframing, improvising, adapting, overcoming;
2. interpersonal: consultation, negotiation, deliberation, conflict resolution, facilitation, brokering, preceptoring, educating, animating, changing roles;
3. enactment: enabling, empowering, responsiveness, creativity;
4. ethics of interconnectiveness and interdependence: removing obstacles, freeing others to act better;
5. staying the course while rocking the boat: imagination, experimentation, responsibility to explore, emphasis on sins of omission, learning by prototyping.[37]

These competencies are not only individual, but collective, in the sense that rules of interaction among individuals generate emerging properties that derive from the dynamics of situations, not from the heads of actors. The 'interaction order' (in the language of Erwin Goffman) generates a sort of collective intelligence, a sort of social mindset.[38]

[36] Jan-Peter Voß, Dierk Bauknecht, René Kemp, (eds). 2006. *Reflexive Governance for Sustainable Development*. Cheltenham: Edward Elgar.

[37] Donald N. Michael. 1993. "Governing by Learning: Boundaries, Myths and Metaphors," *Futures*, 25(1): 81-89.

[38] Erwin Goffman. 1959. *The Presentation of Self in Everyday Life*. New York: Doubleday; Howard Rheingold. 2002. *Smart Mobs*. Cambridge, UK: Perseus.

The dual (individual and collective) competencies/ capacities obviously interact, and are confronted with a context that ignites some capacities and not others, that affords 'action possibilities' and not others. Whether these affordances are real or perceived is of less relevance than the fact that they limit the realm of possibilities.

In particular, the context generates affordances that individuals and collectivities perceive or learn to perceive. "Affordances are not fixed properties: they are relationships that hold between objects and agents ... to discover and make use of affordances is one of the important ways" to deal with novel situations.[39]

Learning to perceive affordances better, or developing ways to improve such perception, is the substance of social learning, and is at the core of innovation and innovative design. This is the way in which the automatic pilot is improved.

Dynamics

The dynamic of stewardship need not result only from the heads of actors: it may equally emerge from the context and situations. The megacommunity, the common knowledge, and the forces of synchronization are all 'enabling resources' at the core of self-organization, and may complement or counter in a substantial way the forces triggered by explicit efforts to influence the nature of the game and to nudge the organization or the social system in certain directions.

Megacommunity

A megacommunity – "a public sphere in which organizations and people deliberately join together around a compelling issue of mutual importance, following a set of practices and principles that will make it easier to achieve results" – entails a requisite amount of both trust (institutional, inter-organizational and interpersonal) and social capital.[40]

---

[39] Donald A. Norman. 1999. "Affordances, Conventions and Design," *Interactions,* 6(3): 38-43; Donald A. Norman. 2007. *The Design of Future Things.* New York: Basic Books, p. 68-69.

[40] Mark Gerencser et al. 2006. "The Mega-Community Manifesto" *strategy + business* (www.strategy-business.com), August 16.

In practice, Gerencser et al. have identified four critical elements for a thriving megacommunity: (1) understanding the problems to be resolved, the necessary players and partners, and the ways in which they affect one another; (2) the presence of partners in a listening, learning and understanding mode; (3) designing and customizing of suitable cross-sector arrangements; and (4) experiments: learning from them, and effective collective monitoring of progress.

People and groups potentially affected by, or involved in, stewardship are by definition players in the megacommunity. For all of them, their interests (and views) will tend to be framed by the mindset that dominates the culture in good currency in the socio-economic context. Their opinions will evolve to some extent as time passes, and will change to a greater or lesser degree as a result of external influences.

Those forces do not necessarily result in convergent interests. In fact, parties may pursue contradictory objectives and engineer dynamic blockages and even sabotage to derail what might appear to an outsider as an emerging agreement on certain value-adding and coordination-strengthening rules or guideposts.

Common knowledge
Another set of forces that is most important in the dynamics of stewardship is common knowledge. Michael Chwe has shown that "coordination is often achieved through adaptation and evolution and implicit communication, but often people explicitly communicate" in order to solve them. Looking at how common knowledge emerges, he shows that it is often through communicative events like rituals, ceremonies and other cultural practices.

He thereby demonstrates how the problem of indeterminacy in coordination can be resolved by common knowledge. It has been shown that persons having agreed to meet in New York or Paris, but with some uncertainty as to where exactly in that city, will draw on their common knowledge of that city to elicit where the meeting is likely to be. It thereby indicates ways in which intervention might nudge people toward coordination through generating common knowledge, and allowing choices to be made by actors on that basis (i.e., allowing self-organization to proceed).[41]

This approach explicitly leverages the cultural and informational contexts likely to generate effective self-organization.

Synchronization

Yet another set of forces at work in the dynamics of stewardship has to do with synchronization: the fact that, for reasons that are not always clear, humans, like animals, would appear to fall into synchronized behaviour in self-organized ways (traffic flows, applause, massive swings in electoral support, mob formation, etc.). Steven Strogatz has thoroughly reviewed the existence of synchronization in animal and human worlds: the spontaneous outbreak of coordinated herd or mob behaviour, with certain thresholds (or mix of thresholds for different groups) defining tipping points where mass synchronization occurs.[42]

Strogatz has shown that, in the animal world, spontaneous coordination is omnipresent (fireflies flashing in unison, flocks of birds flying in formation, etc.). It has also been shown that synchronization occurs in the material world of lifeless things like clocks. In the human world, group-think, coordination of menstrual cycles, etc. are also well documented. In the same way, synchronization materializes in group behaviour, and we are beginning to understand the mechanisms underlying such generation of order out of chaos when certain thresholds are reached. This illustrates in a simple way the forces of self-organization that need to be taken into account.

Such forces of synchronization need not generate orderly coordination. They often generate fibrillation or mobs. But understanding such forces is fundamental if one ever hopes to find the equivalent of a *de*fibrillator at the social level.

---

[41] M.S.W. Chwe. 2001. *Rational Ritual*; see also Thomas C. Schelling. 1978. *Micromotives and Macrobehavior.* New York: Norton.

[42] Steven Strogatz. 2003. *Sync – The Emerging Science of Spontaneous Order.* New York: Hyperion.

Automatic pilot and collibration

The dynamics of stewardship underpinning the metaphor of the automatic pilot need to be understood as a mix of mechanisms, many of which are designed with certain purposes in mind, but many of which are simply the result of self-organization, either triggered by common knowledge or as unintended consequences of context, situations and experimental interventions, or as a result of 'sync'.

This definition of stewardship therefore escapes from the simplistic anthropomorphic images of leadership, by recognizing both the extent to which mechanisms can be put in place (capable of nudging the organization or the social system in preferred directions), and the extent to which experiments with prototypes to tinker with complex non-linear systems are likely to generate important unintended consequences as a result of the self-organization it triggers.

Such an approach does not promise success in governing organizations, but it provides an insight into the ways in which governing works.

This entails the realization of the limited extent to which deliberate strategy and policy can interfere with the ensemble of 'invisible' institutions and mechanisms *de facto* making up the automatic pilot – as a result of the very complexity with which it has to interfere and of the difficulty in intervening effectively in the internal balances of the system without a very good knowledge of how the system works.

In plural, heterogeneous and fractious contexts, subsidies, partnerships and sermons, or legal instruments are often costly and ineffective. An alternative is *collibration* – a process making use of existing tensions and built-in checks and balances of a particular kind of social system, so that a "relatively small use of power, as stick, carrot or sermon, may then tip the balance of the self-policing tensions already manifest."[43] Such an approach requires a good knowledge of how the system works and may prove destabilizing, precarious and transient, and may not be routinizeable, but it is a cheap, non-committing, and unobtrusive form of intervention.

Small interventions may have important effects, but there is no need to count exclusively on government to get involved in collibration. Indeed, in collaborative decentred metagovernance, many co-producers of governance can and, in fact, do collibrate: this underpins the collective production of the automatic pilot.

Putting all this together

The new vistas generated by this new cosmology may appear at first overwhelmingly difficult to grasp because they challenge so many features of the conventional wisdom. But the sort of complexification that is entailed is a necessary corrective to the overly simplistic traditional cosmology that has been the source of much governance failure.

The main drivers of this complexification are the greater complexity of the context and the imperatives of Ashby's law of requisite variety – which states that, for effective regulation, the variety of the regulator must be equal to or greater than the variety of the system being regulated. In our all-connected world, uncertainty thrives and our limited knowledge generates actions pregnant with unintended consequences. The pretence of planners – planning is a word that has the same Latin root as flattening – is both arrogant and groundless. In the face of deep uncertainty and, with the presumption that the unthinkable has to be anticipated, the only effective response is fast and effective adjustment and social learning.

Postulating a world of things and not of processes, segmenting private, public and reciprocity mechanisms,

---

[43] Andrew Dunsire defines it in the following way: "When weights placed in one pan of a letter balance begin to equal the weight of the letter in the other, the scales librate, oscillating around the horizontal. Co-libration means taking a part in this process, introducing a bias or compensator into such a field so that it arrives at a steady state when otherwise it might not" (Andrew Dunsire. 1996. "Tipping the Balance: Autopoiesis and Governance," *Administration & Society* (28): 321).

disingenuously presuming that there is always someone omniscient and fully in charge who can lead in the name of common values, and merrily ignoring the forces of self-organization – has had the great benefit of making this cartoonesque world look as if it might readily be 'governed' by some enlightened leader, but this is a fantasy.

The complexity of the environment calls for modes of intervention that are much more sophisticated. Most issue domains cannot be fully understood in a pluralistic and complex environment, goals are unclear and hardly well defined, and means-ends relationships are quite unstable and unreliable. This explains much policy disingenuity. The policy maker, having defined policy as a bow and arrow game, but being too badly informed to define clear goals and robust means-ends relationships meaningfully, is condemned to missing the moving target; so it becomes tempting to shoot the arrow, and draw a circle around the place where the arrow falls by mischievously redefining the objectives *ex post*.

In the new perspective, governing is a form of inquiry to discover what is going on, and to try, through learning by experimenting, to nudge the organization or the social system ever so slightly in desirable directions.[44]

Collaborative decentred metagovernance recognizes that, in this more complex world, the broader the range of mechanisms at one's disposal, the greater the possibility is of 'designing an inquiring system' that can learn fast and guide more useful interventions.

A central challenge in this sort of world is to recognize the immense forces of the environment that one cannot control, the difficulty of mobilizing all stakeholders for action when their perspectives are so different, and the very absence of any initiative that would truly and quasi-magically 'resolve' such ill-defined problems.

Collaborative decentred metagovernance entails a need to scheme virtuously: (1) first by 'collibration' – experimenting

---

[44] Richard H. Thaler and Cass R. Sunstein. 2008. *Nudge*. New Haven: Yale University Press.

continuously with small initiatives to make the highest and best use of the forces in the context; (2) by 'obliquity' – recognizing that it is often more effective to intervene indirectly and in an oblique way rather than in a frontal and confrontational way;[45] and (3) through *'bricolage'* and tinkering at tipping points where small changes may have important impacts, without triggering the robust opposition of the forces of dynamic conservatism.[46]

This dynamic and opportunistic work to take full advantage of the wave (as a good surfer does) gives the environment its determining place, and obviously makes the governing work more problematic. It becomes even more complex when it is realized that such work cannot be done except with the collaboration of indispensable partners.

Intervening continuously, reflexively, and collaboratively to improve the automatic pilot by developing new capacities, leveraging the contextual forces, and making the highest and best use of networks is immensely more complex than playing the bow-arrow-target game and ratiocinating on marksmanship. But this is what collaborative decentred metagovernance requires.

This new perspective brings governance back into its appropriate territory. Sigmund Freud used to say that there were three impossible tasks – to cure, to educate, and to govern – because in all these cases, nothing can be done without the collaboration of those to whom one is ministering, but this has never stopped medical doctors or educators from trying, and succeeding less and less badly as time goes by. One cannot imagine that meta-governors will not be able to do the same – as the true nature of the challenge they face becomes less opaque.

In the next two chapters, we probe the major ways in which collaborative decentred metagovernance will deploy itself a bit further: into inquiring systems and social learning (chapter 2) and through scheming virtuously (chapter 3).

---

[45] John Kay. 2011. *Obliquity – Why our goals are best achieved indirectly*. New York: The Penguin Press.

[46] Donald A. Schön. 1971. *Beyond the Stable State*. New York: Norton; Ruth Hubbard and Gilles Paquet. 2010. *The Black Hole of Public Administration*. Ottawa: University of Ottawa Press.

CHAPTER 2

| Inquiring Systems

Gilles Paquet and Christopher Wilson

"... an inquiring system has no safe and assured pathway ahead."
– C. West Churchman

Introduction

The notion of governance has helped to identify the broad set of challenges that confront one in designing suitable stewardship for hybrid organizations or broader socio-technical systems in a fractious and turbulent modern world. It has also led to enlightening explorations into the causes and sources of pathologies in the private, public and social sectors,[47] and to some useful probing into the features of effective collaborative decentred metagovernance regimes in all those domains.[48]

However, the approaches to governance in good currency often fail to define precise ways to design effective inquiring and 'wayfinding' systems as the foundations of stewardship capable of ensuring the requisite social learning and the needed collaboration. In particular, they underestimate the

---

[47] Gilles Paquet. 2004. *Pathologies de gouvernance*. Montreal: Liber.
[48] Gilles Paquet. 2011. *Gouvernance collaborative: un antimanuel*. Montreal: Liber.

central importance of developing a repertoire of tools and affordances (helpful devices like checklists) to bolster the dynamic collaborative process of monitoring, reflection and self-adjustment that is needed to provide the requisite trust, process guidance, learning and innovation.

The collaborative decentred metagovernance approach adds value by attempting to develop such a toolbox. It helps practitioners experiment with various protocols in the construction of collaborative regimes capable of ensuring shared learning, commitment and stewardship. It has done so by recombining the whole range of mechanisms that have proved useful in the private, public and social sectors in new innovative ways that align better with the turbulent and chaotic environment of modern organizations, and with the new pluralism of values and beliefs characteristic of diverse populations and stakeholders.

Until now, initiatives on this front have been constrained by three major and inter-related handicaps:

1. a tendency to wallow in the oversimplified stylizations of complex governance systems that were designed for well-structured and stylized problems;

2. a reluctance to abandon worn-out conventional methods (because of the intellectual capital already invested in them) even when they have proven most unhelpful in dealing with the ill-structured problems generated by complex systems and no-one-is-in-charge type organizations; and

3. a propensity to slip into fanciful thinking when it comes to defining the way in which collaboration will materialize – frequently being satisfied to presume that it will come forth automatically, without clearly explaining how it will emerge, or how one can catalyze and nudge this process ahead. This naïve willingness to assume that collaboration will emerge spontaneously, as if by some form of immaculate conception, is so widespread that it led the former U.S. Surgeon General, Jocelyn Elders, to remind all (not without a bit of irony) that, *de facto,*

collaboration continues to be seen "as an un-natural act between non-consenting adults."[49]

Our view is that, first and foremost, one must squarely embrace the full complexity of a world posing ill-structured problems, and agree to dump unhelpful antiquarian tools. Second, to do this, a certain pragmatic mindset is crucial: one that is framed by a 'mode of inquiry' that embraces paradoxes, tolerates multiple perspectives, and indulges in experimentation and serious play with whatever quasi-analytical protocols may be at hand.[50] Finally, in mapping out a workable approach to collaborative decentred metagovernance, one must be neither overly optimistic nor overly pessimistic.[51] Most often, collaboration will not emerge organically: one has to work hard at finding ways to use all the available physical and cognitive affordances that might help people to develop trust and empathy. This can be done by making the highest and best use of the mechanisms of reciprocity instead of relying exclusively, as so many organizations try to do, on coercion and market incentives. However, it would be immensely counter-productive and untrue to presume that collaboration is not practically feasible.[52]

We will proceed in four stages.

First, we succinctly sketch the underlying conceptual framework that has guided our governance work up to now, and hint at the reasons why such a framework requires some modifications if it is to be of use in the construction of an

---

[49] Thomas Backer. 2003. *Evaluating Community Collaborations*. New York: Springer Publishing, p. 10.

[50] Michael Schrage. 2000. *Serious Play*. Boston: Harvard Business Scholl Press; Roger Martin. 2007. *The Opposable Mind*. Boston: Harvard Business School Press.

[51] Yochai Benkler. 2011. *The Penguin and the Leviathan*. New York: Crown Business.

[52] Hayagreeva Rao and Robert Sutton. 2008. "The Ergonomics of Innovation," *The McKinsey Quarterly*, September: 131-141; Martin A. Nowak. 2006. "Five Rules for the Evolution of Collaboration," *Science*, 314 (December): 1560-1563; Martin A. Nowak (with Roger Highfield). 2011. *SuperCooperators*. New York: The Free Press.

inquiring system that requires cooperation triumph over narrow self-interest.

Second, we make the case for inquiring systems as an assemblage of learning heuristics (or practical shortcuts), and for the use of checklists and other devices as affordances, constituting crucial components in a protocol to design and operate a collaborative decentred-metagovernance-based stewardship.

Third, we put forward a provisional checklist of crucial questions that could guide in the production of an effective inquiring system.

Fourth, we make a case for stewardship based on collaboration being neither impossible nor implausible, but rather demonstrably and pragmatically constructible if the powers of reciprocity are better understood and put to use.

In conclusion, we suggest some caution in experimenting with this instrument.

The underlying conceptual framework: sound, but in need of improvement

As discussed earlier in this volume, governance is effective coordination when power, resources, and information are widely distributed among a variety of stakeholders. It bridges silos across organizational sections, and bridges moments across time. A very stylized and succinct definition of this approach might be the study of the needed responses to coordinate and collaborate in the face of twin organizational pressures, from within and without, that emerge:

1. in part as a reaction to the greater diversity within modern organizations and social systems themselves in terms of world views, systems of beliefs and stakeholder capacities – a situation that makes the challenges of arriving at concerted organizational learning and collaborative decentred metagovernance ever more daunting; and

2. in part as a reaction to the greater diversity involved in complex and turbulent environments that forces

organizations and social systems to adjust faster and more effectively to survive.

These forces have challenged the old Big 'G' government approach to decision making (hierarchical, centralized, authoritarian, coercive) in all sectors (private, public and social) in this new turbulent and pluralist world. As described previously, this is because, in our world, (a) nobody is able to fully take charge, and (b) there are no shared values that are agreed to by all stakeholders that might serve as common reference points to guide such top-down decision making.

As a result, an alternative small 'g' governance approach (more pluralist, participative, horizontal and experimentalist) has emerged, that would appear to be better equipped to cope with these polycentric coordination challenges, and more capable of reconciling the variety of belief systems at play into a workable accommodation that takes full advantage of the dispersed information, resources and power, under the control of the different stakeholders. Under small 'g' governance, organizational and governance regimes are predominantly shaped by the dynamics of social learning, which generate the needed coordination and collaboration arrangements through multiple, reflexive learning loops, that are capable of yielding innovation and resilience in an ongoing process of pragmatic value-adding (in the broader sense of the term, not just economic).[53]

In the different terrains where this work has been carried out, a variety of principles and mechanisms have been used (and have proven effective) in designing an architecture of stewardship capable of fostering high-performance collaborative organizations and socio-economic systems: mechanisms such as maximum participation, true prices and costs, subsidiarity, competition, multi-stability,

[53] Gilles Paquet. 1999. *Governance Through Social Learning.* Ottawa: University of Ottawa Press; Gilles Paquet. 1999. "Innovations in Governance in Canada," *Optimum*, 29 (2/3): 71-81.

adequate negotiating forums, moral contracts, fail-safe mechanisms, etc.[54]

But even in the private, public and social spheres, where these principles and mechanisms have been experimented with, all too often collaborative behaviour has been too readily assumed to emerge as a matter of course.

Obviously, it is understood that mutualization and collaboration are essential ingredients for effective stewardship, that trust is its crucial lubricant, and that social learning by trial and error requires serious play with prototypes and experimentation of all sorts. However, our observation has been that too often there is little in the way of systematic protocols to probe how stewardship can be enacted and this process of production of collaboration stimulated.

Yet after so many terrains have been explored, and experiments carried out, it would appear timely to see if one might not be able to derive from such experiences not recipes, but a 'protocol' that could help in designing a path for grappling with the collaborative elements of collaborative decentred metagovernance in an inquiring system, drawing on the mixed mechanisms already available.

Inquiring systems as heuristics and affordances

To be able to do so, one must first examine how the nature of an inquiring system is at the core of modern collaborative decentred metagovernance. We suggest that such a system may be characterized as a 'collaborative search system' that is capable of pulling together the diverse aspirations, knowledge, resources and authorities into a whole. In doing so, it provides the requisite stewardship for ensuring ongoing commitments, learning and experimentation; encourages direction-finding; creates resilience in the face of constant

---

[54] Gilles Paquet. 2008. *Gouvernance : mode d'emploi*. Montreal: Liber; Christopher Wilson and Wayne Foster. 2006. *11 Case Studies of Ontario Community Portals*, an annex to Ruth Hubbard, Gilles Paquet and Christopher Wilson. *Reviewing COPSC: Building on the lessons of community portals*. Report prepared for the Ontario Ministry of Economic Development and Trade, May.

change; and contributes to innovation and productivity increases that will constitute value-adding to society in the broadest sense.

Consistent with the traditional Newtonian view of cause and effect is the notion that 'someone must be in charge,' causing some traditionalists to postulate nothing less than a mechanical 'Grand Designer' that is omniscient, omnipotent, and capable of replacing the human messiness of political haggling and collaboration. Such a command-and-control engine is clearly at odds with the realities of our complex and ever-changing world, where goals are unclear and the connections between 'means' and 'ends' unstable.[55]

Other groups, inspired by quantum perspectives, propose an approach – based less on goals and control, and more on intelligence and innovation – that embraces an intelligence-gathering function, the use of various search processes that make use of social learning processes of reframing and reflecting, and is primarily satisfied with keeping the organization of collective dialogue within a certain corridor, defined by certain mutually agreed upon norms of acceptableness.[56]

This latter approach is a better fit, in our mind, with collaborative decentred metagovernance, as it underpins a process of stewardship based on inquiring systems as assemblages of mechanisms and practices of collaboration and social learning, capable of bolstering the political process of collective decision making by affording it a capacity to avoid avoidable mistakes.

---

[55] Alycia Lee and Tatiana Glad. 2011. *Collaboration: The Courage to Step into a Meaningful Mess.* Amsterdam.collaboracy@the-hub.net, March.

[56] Geoffrey Vickers. 1965. *The Art of Judgment.* London: Methuen; Harold L. Wilensky. 1967. *Organizational Intelligence.* New York: Basic Books. For example, this sort of approach has been used by Carl Taylor to gauge public policy options based on the answer to four probing questions: Is what is being proposed technically feasible? Is it socially acceptable? Is it implementable? Is it too politically destabilizing? Carl A. Taylor. 1997. "The ACIDD Test," *Optimum* 27(4): 53-62.

There may be a variety of ways to proceed along this latter path, but all such approaches can be stylized as proceeding in two stages:

- first, the use of 'fast and frugal heuristics' (rules of thumb or other practical shortcuts that are consciously or unconsciously used by most practitioners) that can be customized for use by specific individuals and groups in specific circumstances; and,

- second, the use of 'affordances' or helpful devices (like the checklists that have been successfully used by pilots for decades as part of their take-off and landing procedures) to help operationalize such heuristics.

Inquiring systems as assemblage of heuristics

An inquiring system is fundamentally about seeking and processing information as a sort of self-organized, direction-finding, 'super automatic pilot.' It is designed to mop up information; to actively seek out anomalies and investigate identifiable pathologies; to explore problem definitions; to seek out potential collaborators; to generate testable prototypes of responses from conversations with those collaborators; to fail early and to fail often using these prototypes, but also to learn quickly and thoroughly from each such experimentation; to disseminate the good and bad news about what has been learned; and to continuously close the knowing-doing gap within the organization or society. In this regard, an inquiring system meets the learning challenge of collaborative decentred metagovernance by assembling the most appropriate heuristics to match problems with the existing context and available knowledge, resources and power capabilities in the least amount of time.

An inquiring system is not simply an evolving repository of knowledge or data, but it is also an evolving nexus of relationships among partners and contributors that is continually being transformed by the information being accumulated. Those relationships are not necessarily etched in memorandums of understanding (MOUs) or formal partnership agreements (as some would have us believe) but in the willing co-learning and value-adding exchanges that the relationships engender. Consequently, the various relationships (internal and external, quantitative and qualitative, functional and metabolic, etc.) are continually transforming both the intelligence-gathering processes and the implementing capabilities that they mediate. Yet the focus of an inquiring system must always remain in the corridor of the feasible – to ensure its outcomes are both desirable and viable, as defined by its relevant constraints, of which threat-avoidance is one.

As a result, any inquiring system is naturally the result of a cumulative process of both learning and unlearning, especially when the partner interactions may cause a deconstruction of assumptions, frames and the sense of what is possible. System outputs are subsequently compiled and acted upon through a self-referential system of modification, development and redefinition over time. This learning and unlearning cycle is best facilitated by discovery engines that are frugal and flexible, that are based on learning by trial and error, but that have no guarantee of success in a world that is constantly changing.

For example, if someone has lost her pen in a room, she could work 'backward' from where she is, or start where she entered the room and work 'forward' until she finds it. Or if that does not work, she could 'associate' where she was when she last recalled having it. All these strategies are not as certain of producing results as the algorithmic approach of walking around the room in a grid search pattern, but the less certain heuristic approach is more likely to produce results much sooner.[57]

---

[57] David Straus (*How to Make Collaboration Work Powerful Ways to Build Consensus, Solve Problems and Make Decisions*. San Francisco: Berrett-Koehler, 2002) identifies dozens of such heuristics that are regularly used in the practice of collaboration. They are grouped into eight categories, and each heuristic is conceptualized as a pair of active verbs which represent alternatives, although not necessarily opposite, approaches to tackling the problem. For a review of those strategies, an examination of their powers and limitations, and some exercises demonstrating how the ability to make use of them can be developed, see David Straus. 1972. *Strategy Notebook: Tools for Change*. San Francisco: Interaction Associates.

Consequently, effective collaborative decentred meta-governance will inevitably create and make use of a large repertoire of these fast and frugal heuristics as part of its inquiring systems. The choice of heuristics is usually matched to particular issue domains and partnership features, allowing partners to compose an inquiring system that is both consistent with their capabilities and ecologically rational – well matched with their environment. Heuristics are made of combinations of skills, abilities, practices, techniques, or gimmicks which have become adopted because they are effective for those who use them. For instance, a 'tit-for-tat' heuristic,[58] comprised of the abilities to cooperate, to forget, and to imitate,[59] might be particularly useful among partners with low trust levels, but less useful among partners with long histories of cooperation.

In most metagovernance regimes, such practical abilities, skills and mechanisms are the critical factors for collaborative success. Consequently, ensuring that these abilities are in place and well developed must become an important feature of a successful inquiring system. Sadly, these cooperative abilities and skills are not commonly encouraged. However, the growing need for effective collaboration is increasing both the demand for effective affordances and their value, as they can help to stimulate the right and timely use of skills to facilitate more cooperative behaviour.

Affordances

Affordances are physical or cognitive devices designed to lower the cost of thinking, to create space for people to think more clearly about things, to take collective decisions, and then to engage in joint action on that basis, more easily. These are devices that afford certain action possibilities and not

---

[58] This is the well tested game theory heuristic of cooperating first, then imitating your partner's last behaviour (cooperation or non-cooperation), while keeping in mind only their last move and forgetting all previous moves.

[59] Gerd Gigerenzer. 2001. "The Adaptive Toolbox" in G. Gigerenzer and R. Selten, (eds). *Bounded Rationality – The Adaptive Toolbox*. Cambridge, MA: The MIT Press, p. 37-50.

others. Such devices are meant to help focus individual and collective attention on key issues, and therefore expedite the use of appropriate heuristics in navigating the waters of shared commitment in partner management.[60]

As mentioned earlier, checklists are one very good example of what we mean by affordances: they are a fast and frugal way to focus the mind and attention on key issues. They do not provide answers or ways to generate answers, but they do ensure that key questions are asked. They are like the doors to a building. They provide access, but with no guarantee of finding what one is seeking or the means to find it once inside. In this way, they afford some effectiveness in coordination or collaboration in complex situations by ordaining that certain fundamental questions be addressed. Then, coupled with strategies to deal with such questions, they can afford support for collaborative governance by strengthening the work of its inquiring system.

The effectiveness of checklists as a facilitator of collaboration has been demonstrated in many areas. Atul Gawande, for instance, documented the use of checklists for helping surgical teams to effectively and efficiently steward the collaborative activities of operating room teams.[61]

In practice, checklists tend to evolve as social learning progresses, and as new experiences and new contexts materialize. In the aircraft industry, for instance, manufacturers constantly update their cockpit checklists to reflect recent pilot and aviation industry experiences with the aircraft, together

---

[60] Ruth Hubbard and Gilles Paquet. 2010. *The Black Hole of Public Administration*. Ottawa: University of Ottawa Press, p. 213-216.

[61] Atul Gawande. 2009. *The Checklist Manifesto*. New York: Metropolitan Books. The results, when applied to the operating rooms, were phenomenal as revealed by the results of an eight-city pilot study that was carried out. Complications dropped by 36%, operating room deaths fell by 47%, infections originating in the operating room dropped by almost half (Gawande 2009: 154). Further, analyses of exit surveys of staff members coming out of surgery also helped uncover the key causal mechanism that explained why the checklist approach had been so successful. As it turned out, the key factor was that the use of checklists caused a significant increase in the level of communication among operating room collaborators.

with new regulations. In fact, a publication date is stamped on all their checklists to ensure that only the most up-to-date version is used with each new flight.

The use of operating room checklists was itself inspired by the use of the same affordance by the aircraft pilots in the cockpit.

*   *   *

In closing this section, since we have introduced a number of important new concepts, it might be useful to summarize our argument.

In the face of ever more complex, turbulent and novelty-generating contexts, collaborative decentred metagovernance aims at providing the requisite coordination through evolving inquiring systems that embrace intelligence and innovation by developing capacities for both social learning and collaboration. As tools of stewardship, inquiring systems stimulate collaborative 'wayfinding' through a *mélange* of mechanisms that make the highest and best use of frugal heuristics, which are, in turn, operationalized by affordances that help individuals or groups to focus their attention in certain ways, thereby affording certain action possibilities and not others.

Collaborative decentred metagovernance (having shown the hollowness of leadership) is, therefore, built on the much more practical and pragmatic approach to stewardship, which arises as the product of an assemblage of inquiring systems. These inquiring systems are, in turn, made up of assemblages of mechanisms, rules of thumb, practices and skill sets that foster 'wayfinding' and collaboration in healthy environments of experimentation and serious play.

Collaborative decentred metagovernance represents more of an umbrella concept for defining the multiplex nature of the new governing model, while stewardship is the process in which that shared governance becomes embodied through processes of 'wayfinding' and collaborative social learning. To return to our 'super-automatic pilot' metaphor, inquiring systems, and their mechanisms, heuristics and affordances, are the mechanical components underpinning stewardship. They are ways to build the requisite relationships to help individuals and groups go through their social learning with minimal avoidable errors.

Collaborative decentred metagovernance as inquiring systems

The practice of stewardship in collaborative decentred metagovernance is, in essence, a complex orchestration of interacting inquiring systems – a set of processes to ensure effective coordination in the different sectors when power, resources and information are widely distributed. They are drawn from the whole arsenal of mechanisms developed around coercion, market exchanges and reciprocity. The inquiring system is the means by which stewardship is enacted among participating partners to help shape collective purpose and performance. Stewardship therefore provides the collaborative glue that involves trust building, promoting shared authority and commitment, fostering co-learning, mediating joint decision making, and ensuring shared accountability, etc.

Inquiring systems may not be the same in each of the private, public and social spheres, nor in every issue domain, any more than the same style of coat is required to protect people from the elements. But, in whatever sphere or issue domain a cooperative endeavour operates, there are common challenges that will confront the designers of inquiring systems as they are used to enable stewardship and achieve effective collaborative governance.

One can broadly outline the key stages in the development of collaborative metagovernance as responses to four questions:
- Does the situation need changing?
- What is the problem?
- How can we work together?
- How can we learn together and evaluate our progress?

These questions should allow the designer to fashion an approach to collaboration in four phases, as depicted in Figure 2 below.

FIGURE 2. Four Phases for Designing Collaborative Decentred Metagovernance

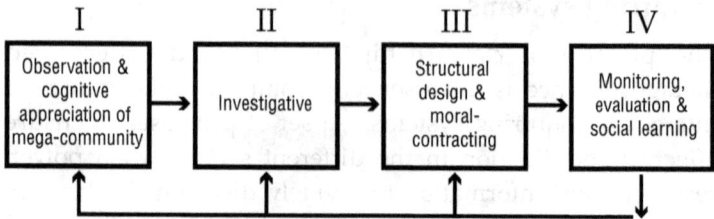

The first phase is primarily 'observational and cognitive': the particular issue domain is examined to determine its 'fit' with the megacommunity involved.[62] In the process, one would explore whether there are any detectable anomalies present; what features of the issue domains are salient; what causal mechanisms are at work; and who are the primary stakeholders (that hold such a significant amount of power, resources and information that they need to be profoundly involved in any process intent on designing or redesigning the collaborative governance regime).[63]

The second phase is 'investigative', focusing on defining the problem and the task at hand more precisely: the non-negotiable constraints imposed by the megacommunity or by the ethos of the milieu;[64] the nature of the value-adding anticipated; and the harms to be avoided, if at all possible, in the process of generating and implementing solutions. In this way, partners can begin contributing to the construction of the upper and lower bounds of what is to be accomplished (at best or minimally) by their work together. And simultaneously, they

[62] Mark Gerencser et al. 2008. *Megacommunities*. New York: Palgrave Macmillan.

[63] Operating under the principle of inclusivity, less significant stakeholders could also be involved, but in a less profound and significant way and at times of their choosing.

[64] As in the case of Carl Taylor's four norms to gauge public policies.

can begin identifying the nature and distribution of risks and other material, financial, human, psychic and emotional costs, together with the distribution of potential rewards and benefits, both tangible and intangible.

The third phase is a 'structural-design-cum-moral-contracting' phase that unfolds in two parallel, but intricately integrated sub-processes that identify how partners will work together, while putting in place the necessary social capital to support that work.

The first sub-process concerns the development of the institutional/organizational structures (legal, informational, etc.) that will ensure that the necessary rules of the game required for any collaboration are viable. This also concerns the choice of instruments, arrangements and affordances that will be necessary to foster social learning sufficiently to allow at least a modicum of chance of early successes, and provide a foundation for future, more ambitious achievements.

The second sub-process – working in parallel – concerns trust conventions and moral contracts, but also legal arrangements and incentive-reward systems that need to be put in place to mobilize the willing collaboration of all the significant stakeholders, and to ensure that the requisite *affectio societatis*[65] is developed, so that the collaborative behaviours can last as long as needed.

While the first sub-process defines the structures through which the collaborative activities can flow, the second sub-process encourages a culture of collaboration and trust.

The fourth phase is an 'evaluative and social learning' one: it focuses not strictly on outputs and outcomes (as some might

---

[65] This is a French legal concept in Latin garb that means that two or more people personally and jointly commit themselves to achieving the purpose(s) of their association. French courts have added to objective partnership criteria an indispensable subjective one: the presence of a "spirit of cooperation" among the partners or *affectio societatis*, which defines their willingness to pursue their goals together. Lack of *affectio societatis* is a sufficient condition for the partnership to be dissolved (Vincent Cuisinier. 2008. *L'affectio societatis*. Montpellier: LITEC).

expect in summative evaluations of goals-and-control style approaches), but also on whether the processes of generating collective intelligence and innovation functions have performed well, and whether the collaborative relationships have been sustained and strengthened.

For instance, while the transformation of a complex socio-economic system may take some time to generate summative results, building and maintaining positive partner and stakeholder relationships represents a prerequisite for the future outputs from their collaborative interaction and, therefore, its presence represents a clear interim measure of progress.

This emphasis on transformative capacity (i.e., co-learning and progressivity), and on the changes in the stakeholders' attitudes and behaviours, allows stakeholders to consciously improve both the processes and outcomes of their work together.[66]

Lastly in this fourth phase, there must be additional (though not necessarily formal) mechanisms of conflict resolution to bridge the differences of opinion and interpretation that will inevitably emerge. These, together with 'fail-safe' mechanisms, in case those differences prove irreconcilable, will help provide an antidote for uncooperative behaviours. One, however, should not neglect the potential for sabotage and conflict, and the social traps that may lie beneath the surface of any collaborative venture.[67] There is a danger that behind polite discourse there are threats to the social learning process and even to the organization or the social system.

Installing these safeguards is meant to protect the inquiring systems from being derailed or locked, thereby preventing

[66] Jamie A.A. Gamble. 2008. *A Developmental Evaluation Primer*. Montreal: The J.W. McConnell Family Foundation; Michael Quinn Patton. 2010. *Developmental Evaluation: Applying Complexity Concepts to Enhance Innovation and Use*. New York: Guilford Publications.

[67] Bo Rothstein. 2005. *Social Traps and the Problem of Trust*. Cambridge, UK: Cambridge University Press.

blockages to the gingering of the social learning cycle. The forms of these safeguards may differ ('fail-safe' when the probability of failing is predictably low, and 'safe-fail' when the probability of failing is very high), but they play a key role in sustaining the learning cycle and, consequently, in the effectiveness of the monitoring-evaluation phase.

These four basic phases of collaboration design as illustrated in Figure 3 lead us to consider four sets of stylized questions that are likely to confront any designer of an inquiring system who attempts to steward a collaborative organization or a socio-technical system.

FIGURE 3.

An Inquiring Process for Collaborative Governance

In Figure 4, each of the columns aligns with the four phases in designing collaborative governance, and is itself the locus of a large number of related questions. Each of the columns is also the source of an array of fast and frugal rules of thumb and affordances that can be designed to provide answers to these questions as well as many others.

Figure 4. Provisional Checklist of Questions

I Does the situation need changing?	II What is the problem?	III How will you work together?	IV How will you learn together & evaluate your progress?
1. Are there any detectable anomalies?	6. What is the task at hand?	a. DESIGN	12. What feedback & informational loops do you have to enable social learning
2. What are the salient features of the issue domain?	7. What are the non-negotiable constraints within the mega-community?	10. What instruments of collaboration and social learning can you use to produce short term success and long term commitment?	13. What collective learning processes do you have in place?
3. What are the causal mechanisms at play?	8. Who are the stakeholders that must be included and how will you involve them?	b. CONVENTIONS	14. How will you gauge ongoing performance objectively?
4. Can this be resolved by a single actor?	9. What are the risks and potential rewards, and how will these be aligned among the various partners?	11. What are the conventions & moral contracts that need to be negotiated to maintain a culture of collaboration?	15. How will you gauge changes in attitudes & behaviours among partners?
5. Who are the key stakeholders?			16. How will you resolve conflicts?
			17. What safe-fail mechanisms are in place?
			18. At what point would you dissolve the collaboration?

As new information becomes available or new circumstances materialize, the constant process of inquiry fuels the cycle of social learning, innovation, shared commitment and mutual accountability. The checklist of questions presented above is meant to help kick-start the process of defining the burden of office for each key stakeholder in the collaborative metagovernance process, and afford them the opportunity to reflect on guiding assumptions, structures, technology, or even the theory of what the 'collective enterprise' is all about.

As Donald Schön has shown, theory, structure and technology are in constant interaction in any social system or organization, and social learning may proceed either well or not, depending on the degree of misalignment among the three.[68] Figures 2, 3 and 4 are presented as illustrations of a budding inquiring system likely to trigger social learning and generate collective intelligence and knowledge at three levels: among individual stakeholders, within particular inquiring systems, and among inquiring systems within collaborative decentred metagovernance.

While it is important to note that although each phase is important, phase IV is possibly the most important (and therefore the questions attached to this phase are more crucial) because it determines the tonus of the social learning cycle: the more robust, open, and 'developmental' phase IV is, the more vibrant the learning and, therefore, the inquiring system. Moreover, the more attention given to 'relational learning', the more likely it is that the learning cycle will not become impaired.

Stewardship: self-governance, collibration and collaboration

The processes of inquiring, social learning and 'wayfinding' are underpinned by the collaborative mechanisms that are essential ingredients provided by effective stewardship. But stewardship is not the only source of collaboration. There are, in fact, several.

[68] Donald A. Schön. 1971. *Beyond the Stable State*. New York: Norton.

Sometimes collaboration emerges from self-organization and self-governance, combined with the dynamics of environment and context. It has been shown by Elinor Ostrom and her team, for instance, that this is not only possible but that there is empirical evidence that individuals and groups can develop credible commitments without relying on external authorities.[69] This does not mean that there will always be collaboration, but the Hobbesian prediction that there will be no cooperation – ever – is untenable. It has been shown that, with sufficient information, in an arena where authentic dialogue can occur, together with some monitoring and sanctioning, collaboration can resolve major 'tragedies-of-the-commons-type' problems and other collective challenges.[70]

Moreover, there is the possibility for key institutional partners (or even peripheral ones) at certain moments (as part of their burden of office) to intervene through *bricolage* to catalyze these more organic processes, and to use whatever capacity they may have opportunistically and temporarily to 'collibrate', that is, to tinker with these self-governance processes and to nudge the organization or the social system into a preferred direction faster. This is not a unique privilege of the state: any partner may have the opportunity to do so on occasion, even if there is no necessity for it to happen. It is the transitory nature of this type of intervention that distinguishes it from the ongoing acts of stewardship.

More important, in terms of stewardship, is the possibility of collaboration to allow networks to crystallize into communities of practice, capable of generating cooperation that is neither a result of market incentives or external coercion, but is a result of various forces rooted in reciprocity. The case has been made quite persuasively that cooperation and collaboration do work, and are effective in contexts where traditional management fails, and that even mass collaboration is not only possible, but

---

[69] Elinor Ostrom et al. 1992. "Covenants with and without a Sword: Self-governance is possible," *The American Political Science Review*, 86(2): 404-417.

[70] Adam Kahane. 2004. *Solving Tough Problems*. San Francisco: Berrett-Koehler Publishers.

demonstrably successful.[71] The question, then, is to consider how to ensure that the highest and best use is made of self-organization and of designing for cooperation – through the various collaborative mechanisms of communication, reframing, conventions and moral contracts, and, most importantly, through the use of developmental evaluation.[72]

Developmental evaluation focuses on *ex ante* performance preview rather than on *ex post* performance review. It is well adjusted to experimentation and serious play with prototypes, and contributes meaningfully to an acceleration of the process of social learning, and ongoing 'wayfinding.' It is based on real-time emergent evaluation, and it is geared to accompany and catalyze ongoing development, to adjust general principles to new contexts, to the development of rapid responses, and to deal with major changes like 'black swan events.'[73] Developmental evaluation is a major driver of the sort of apparatus required at the monitoring and learning stage of the reflective process described in box IV in Figure 2 – the portion of the process that is pivotal in social learning.

This catalytic function of stewardship depends fundamentally on harnessing the genetic-cultural evolution of human reciprocity instead of relying exclusively on self-interest and coercion.[74] But the mix of forms of collaboration (more or less explicit, more or less dependent on common knowledge, synchronicity or the like) will depend on the context, and so will the relative importance of design and *bricolage* in relation to the forces of self-governance. What is clear is that the automatic pilot needs to rely on the human propensity to collaborate, as well as on incentives to do so, and to-date, these have been ignored to a greater extent than they should have been.

---

[71] Yochai Benkler, 2011. Don Tapscott and Anthony D. Williams. 2006. *Wikinomics*. New York: Portfolio.

[72] See Yochai Benkler, 2011, chapter 10; and also Michael Quinn Patton. 2011. *Developmental Evaluation*. New York: The Guilford Press.

[73] Nassim Nicholas Taleb. 2007. *The Black Swan – the impact of the highly improbable*. New York: Random House.

[74] Samuel Bowles and Herbert Gintis. 2011. *A Cooperative Species – Human Reciprocity and its Evolution*. Princeton, NJ: Princeton University Press.

A word of warning

The key rationale behind the use of a checklist as an affordance of collaborative decentred metagovernance is that not only do governance failures occur, but that such failures are 'bound to' occur as they do in most human activities.[75]

This means that putting in place casual 'fail-safe' mechanisms in case collaboration does not work will not suffice, in and of itself. Such fail-safe precautions presume that cooperative arrangements or complex policies will generally work: they are included to deal with the most unlikely event that collaboration might fail. Accordingly, the work to develop mature collaborative structures and cultures is not taken very seriously.

If one were to presume that in all likelihood things *will* fail at some point (a presumption consistently supported by experience), then one has to shift from a 'fail-safe' to a 'safe-fail' approach, where attention is directed towards catching the quasi-certain or highly probable failure as soon as possible, in order to minimize the damages that are bound to occur.[76]

From this perspective, the main contribution of affordances is in the prevention of harms that could result from failed partnerships, un-integrated or too narrowly defined policies, under- or un-utilized resources, and a wasteful adversarial environment – all echoes of poor collaborative decentred metagovernance.

As an additional caution, accepting the challenge of being guided by an inquiring system does not mean that one should abandon oneself to the caprices of this system. Any experiment (including that of an inquiring system) entails vigilance and some capacity to resort to nudging action, if and when the inquiring system gives signs of acting in an untoward manner. Yet our observation is that experimentation and prototyping are not a regular feature of traditional governing styles. This

---

[75] Paul Ormerod. 2005. *Why Most Things Fail*. London: Faber & Faber; Henry Petroski. 2006. *Success Through Failure – The Paradox of Design*. Princeton, NJ: Princeton University Press.

[76] C.S. (Buzz) Holling. 1976. "Resilience and Stability of Ecosystems" in Eric Jantsch, C.H. Waddington, (eds). *Evolution and Consciousness in Transition*. Reading, MA: Addison-Wesley, p. 73-92.

reluctance to experiment will only be overcome if there is a culture of experimentation that becomes commonly accepted, and if the notion of affordances as guides is accompanied by assurances that any missteps resulting from experimentation will not lead to the usual blame game, but to organizational learning and quick, corrective action.

Yet even if such a culture existed, we suspect it would be insufficient for the incremental successes with inquiring systems to offset the prevalence of risk aversion that is so pervasive and endemic, particularly in the public sector. For that to occur, we suspect that there will have to be some re-assurances made to those interested in nudging the system that disaster will not be an outcome of these sorts of experiments in social learning. Happily, one of the major advantages of inquiring systems is that, as the processes which comprise robust, continuous vigilance, they are much more likely to catch very small variations in real time before they evolve into major catastrophes. And so, even for those who may be quite risk averse, small experiments with the design of collaborative metagovernance can yield potentially significant benefits.

Anderson and Simister have further suggested that there are rules for running such experiments that can help give the process even more legitimacy and support. They suggest:

- focusing on individuals and thinking short-term to begin with;
- trying unusual, 'out-of-the-box' thinking;
- measuring from the outset, as much as possible, anything that matters;
- being on the lookout for natural experiments of the type that the environment is constantly turning out.

In other words, they suggest that partner vigilance has to be active and ongoing in order to identify what is working, or what could potentially work in any endeavour supported by social learning.[77]

---

[77] Eric T. Anderson and Duncan Simister. 2011. "A step-by-step guide to smart business experiments," *Harvard Business Review*, 89(3): 98-105.

Yet as a steward, one would also have to be vigilant and on the lookout for any obstacles or barriers that may present themselves in the way of establishing an inquiring system – obstacles that may emerge either from without or within the organization or the socio-economic system. The more alert these monitoring mechanisms are, the sooner any anomaly can be detected and, therefore, the faster corrective adjustments can be nudged. This will result in a more effective inquiring system that can act as the engine of good collaborative metagovernance.

It would seem that this etiquette of active and defensive alertness, therefore, serves as the underlying characteristic of inquiring systems, and as the most important capacity of a 'safe-fail' apparatus.

Conclusion

So far, in all the fields where they have been used, heuristics, checklists and other affordances, etc. have been developed primarily by practitioners and from experience over time. They evidently do not need to be theorized first. Indeed, this effort to produce or invent affordances is a common thread emerging from the experience of various practitioners.

While we have attempted to paint a conceptual landscape of inquiring systems and affordances, the real test comes in the field. We have also tried to identify a checklist as collaborative affordance. But, at the moment, all this can be regarded as only a skeletal and indicative prototype. Before such a prototype can be realistically applied in a particular issue domain, there is much in terms of flesh, blood, nerves, muscles, etc., that will have to be added to this skeleton through extensive practitioner conversations.

The same must be said about the design of families of inquiring systems that may be adjusted to particular issue domains: the road to collaborative decentred metagovernance is bound to be paved with inquiring systems and affordances, but much work remains to be done before the new paradigm is fully operational.[78]

---

[78] Gilles Paquet. 2007. "Organization Design as Governance's Achille's Heel," *www.governancia.com*, 1(3): 1-11.

CHAPTER 3

| Scheming Virtuously

Gilles Paquet

"...bringing people together
to make something different happen."
– *Harlan Cleveland*

Introduction

Broadly-speaking, an organization – and, therefore, an inquiring system to steward it – may be represented by a useful acronym – PARC – a mix of *people* or P (stakeholders of all sorts, with their skills, talents and responsibilities), *architecture* or A (relationships of all sorts, defined by the organization charts and the like), *routines* or R (process, policies and procedures), and *culture* or C (shared beliefs, language, norms and mindsets).[79] At any time, these components (PARC) are assembled in various ways, and bound together by ligatures, making them into a more or less coherent whole. Any shock or disturbance in any of these components, whether originating within or without the organization and whether it modifies a physical or a symbolic dimension, obviously triggers some re-

[79] John Roberts. 2004. *The Modern Firm : Organizational Design for Performance and Growth*. Oxford, UK: Oxford University Press.

alignment in all the other dimensions. Thus, the organization continually evolves.

Organizations, therefore, are assemblages constantly undermined (above ground and underground) as a result of the action of new or transformed stakeholders, new emerging relationships, new procedures, or changes in the material or symbolic order. The role of the collaborative decentred metagovernance inquiring system is to intervene in real time in an existing assemblage, to improve the four-dimensional configuration of the organization in a manner that generates better dynamic performance and resilience, given the nature of the environment in which the organization operates, and also taking into account its turbulence and its evolution.

These four dimensions may be tweaked in a creative way to provide effective dynamic coordination. This sort of work requires: (1) a new vocabulary, because critical description is crucial at the diagnostic phase; (2) a new process of experimentalism-based creative thinking; and (3) a new type of competencies to do this work. Moreover, it requires (4) windows of opportunity to 'tinker' with the organization with a modicum of chances of success – at a time and in a way that prevents these efforts from being neutralized by the dynamic conservatism of those who benefit from the existing order. This often requires exceptional circumstances. Otherwise, the pressures of those confronted with real and substantial losses in the short term will trump the timid actions of those hoping for uncertain future benefits from a new order.

However, this process will lead to nothing substantial unless one has been able to have access to, or to develop a mental tool box of levers capable of guiding the work of crafting the inquiring systems. Because this design work is akin to creating a new world, none of the above will suffice unless the design process truly discloses a coherent world (a body), and contributes to imparting to it a style (a soul) that provides it with focal points that underpin purposeful action in pursuit of change.

Given these conditions, it is hardly surprising that such work is eschewed, and that so many organizations are so poorly metagoverned. It is much easier to focus one's attention on less daunting tasks, and to allow poorly-designed automatic pilots to survive, even though the inquiry systems may be the most important determinants of an organization's success.

The rest of the chapter looks at the different ways in which one might be able to interfere effectively with the inquiring systems in real time ('scheming virtuously') by first roughly mapping the process of inquiring; second, by sorting out the different tasks to be tackled; third, by probing the different phases in the crystallization of the inquiring system; and fourth, by hinting at the sort of constraints imposed by having to stay within an ethical corridor, and suggesting how this can be done. These different perspectives on the challenges of 'scheming virtuously' are meant to reveal the diverse pressure points where nudging interventions might be possible and potentially fruitful.

Inquiring system as design challenge

The design process is difficult and elusive, like the pragmatic inquiry of professionals in their practice. However, it is a search process that must be anchored in a loose protocol if it is to serve as a launching pad for experiments and serious play as basic components of the social learning process.

The Simons model as a possible template

A loose protocol or analytical framework is nothing more than a sort of preliminary arrangement of the objects of the inquiry. It provides not a theory of design, but only a set of questions that underpins the appreciation of the situation, and helps in the structuring of the process of construction for performing and resilient inquiring systems.

Robert Simons has proposed a template, based on four basic questions that might be reformulated in the following way: [80]

1) **Stakeholder definition.** What are the best possible assemblages (those that are the most effective and

[80] Robert Simons. 2005. *Levers of Organization Design*. Boston: Harvard Business School Press.

resilient, and likely to serve the organization partners, clients, etc. best)?

2) **Performance variables.** What are the most effective diagnostic systems (the various mechanisms likely to best monitor the organization and to suggest ways to excite it)?

3) **Creative tension resolution.** What are the best mechanisms to resolve the creative tensions between the frames of mind of the different layers and rings of partners in the organization and likely to catalyze interactive networks?

4) **Commitment to others.** What are the mechanisms of shared responsibilities and commitment to others that will ensure some coherence, and the requisite mix of reliability and innovation?

The answers to these questions are meant to help define the four basic dimensions of the Simons framework: (1) the span of control (who should decide?), (2) the span of accountability (tradeoffs in performance measures when it comes to rendering of accounts), (3) the span of influence (the full nature of the interactions and the degree of mobilization they entail), and (4) the span of support (the full range of shared responsibilities).

Simons suggests that the proper alignment for the inquiring system requires that the spans of control (hard) and support (soft) – on the supply side of resources – be adequate to meet the obligations imposed by the spans of accountability (hard) and influence (soft) – on the demand side of resources.

The right organizational design is unlikely to be available ready-made, off the shelf, or off a paradigm. It must be invented, creatively etched on the basis of the properties and capabilities available, but also taking into account context and circumstances.

The central challenge is to find the right balance of reliability and innovation, between exploitation and exploration. This may need to take different forms and may entail different balances depending on the context. But whatever the constraints may be, the focus needs to be on a design that fits well the particular circumstances with which one is faced.

Helping to shape the inquiring systems requires from the co-producers of governance nothing less than a new way of thinking.[81]

Experimentalism and serious play in a dynamic world

A promising way of developing the requisite inquiring systems may be not to impose them 'cold' on any assemblage, but to allow them to emerge once the nature of relevant prototypes is ascertained on the basis of the non-negotiable constraints.

The key to this evolution on the basis of prototypes is:

- a drift toward open source governance (i.e., a form of governance that, as much as possible, enables each partner to have access to the 'code' and to tinker freely with the way the system works, within certain well-accepted constraints); and

- a priority is given to serious play (i.e., a premium on experimentation with imperfect prototypes that one might be able to improve by retooling, restructuring and reframing innovatively and productively).

By partitioning the overall terrain into issue domains and communities of meaning or communities of fate (i.e., assemblages of people united in their common concern for shared problems, or a shared passion for a topic or set of issues), it is possible to identify a vast number of sub-games, each requiring specific treatment. Each issue domain (health, education, environment, etc.) is multifaceted, and is dealt with on an *ad hoc* basis with a view to allowing an idiosyncratic inquiring system design and a stewardship of its own to emerge.

This open system takes into account the people with a substantial stake in the issue domain, the resources available and the culture in place, and allows experiments to shape the required mix of principles and norms, of rules and decision-making procedures likely to promote the preferred mix of

---

[81] A.G.L. Romme. 2003. "Making a Difference: Organization as Design," *Organization Science*, 14(5): 569.

efficiency, resilience and learning. A template likely to be of use across the board may not be available yet, but that does not mean that a workable one cannot be elicited, *hic et nunc*.[82]

It is not sufficient to ensure open access, however; one must also ensure that the appropriate motivations are nurtured so that all partners are willing and able to engage in serious play (i.e., become truly producers of governance through tinkering with the governance apparatus within certain limits).

This, in turn, requires that an amount of collaboration and trust prevails, and calls for a reconfiguration of metagovernance – taking communities of meaning seriously. Such an approach may not only suggest that very different arrangements are likely to emerge from place to place, but would underline the importance of regarding any such arrangement as essentially temporary. The ground is in motion, and diversity is likely to acquire new faces, so different patterns of organizational design are likely to emerge.

This new way of thinking requires that formal or binding arrangements be revisited, played with, and adjusted to open the door to the design of more complex and innovative arrangements likely to deal more effectively with deeper diversity.

Prototyping would appear to be the main activity underpinning serious play:

- identifying some top requirements as quickly as possible;
- putting in place a quick-and-dirty provisional medium of co-development;
- allowing as many interested parties as possible to get involved as partners in improving the arrangement;
- encouraging iterative prototyping; and

[82] Open-source governance does not mean "anything goes" and coercion equals zero. Governments would continue to enact new laws and provide basic services. However, conventional approaches based on the old "plan and push" mentality and one-size-fits-all are bound to become anachronistic (Don Tapscott and Anthony D. Williams. 2010. *Macrowikinomics – Rebooting Business and the World*. Toronto: Portfolio). This approach would be replaced by more participative and collaborative ways to experiment – pilot projects, cooperative ventures, community experiments, etc.

- thereby encouraging all, through playing with prototypes, to get a better understanding of the problems, of their priorities, and of themselves.[83]

The purpose of the exercise is to create a dialogue (creative interaction) between people and prototypes. This may even be more important than creating dialogue among people alone. It is predicated on a culture of active participation that would need to be nurtured.

The sort of democratization of inquiring-system design that ensues and the sort of playfulness that is required for serious play with prototypes are essential for the process to succeed, and they apply equally well to narrow or broad organizational concerns.

Tasks to be tackled

Collaborative decentred metagovernance uses a variety of mechanisms to help institute a living organization that has the capacity to be reliable and innovative, to be resilient but to learn. It aims at coherence, but mainly at dynamism. This cannot be accomplished by tinkering only with the 'hard' dimensions of the organization (architecture and routines); it must also use and shape behaviour and culture.

Principles and mechanisms

Some principles have proven useful in this sort of work:
- maximum participation to ensure tapping into all the relevant knowledge and more collaboration;
- subsidiarity, or the delegation of decision making to the most local level possible;
- some competition to squeeze out organizational slack and promote innovation; and
- multi-stability, that is, the partitioning of the organization into sub-systems, so as to be able to delegate to the one most able to handle a shock or perturbation of the task of doing so, without the other sub-systems being forced to transform.

[83] Michael Schrage. 2000. *Serious Play*. Boston, MA: Harvard Business School Press, p. 199ff.

As for the most useful mechanisms, they have been:

- the setting up of ever more inclusive forums for effective multilogue;
- the negotiation of moral contracts defining well, yet informally, the mutual expectations of the different partners;
- the design of learning loops, enabling the partners to revise their choices of means as the experience unfolds; also enabling them to revise the very ends pursued through reframing the organization when it proves necessary; and
- the invention of fail-safe mechanisms to ensure that the multilogue does not degenerate into meaningless consensuses or stalemates, and to prevent *saboteurs* from derailing the collective effort.

Getting the right fit and sequence

Nadler and Tushman have suggested a blueprint and sequence for inquiring-system design that might serve as a security blanket.[84] Their work might be stylized as follows, taking much liberty with their own sequencing, and taking into account our earlier analyses:

- organizational assessment: functioning, performance gaps
- design criteria: what the new design should accomplish
- groupings: options for general grouping
- coordination requirements: information-processing needs
- linking: linking mechanisms (formal and informal)
- properties and capabilities of the ensuing assemblages
- provisional analysis of impacts
- simulation of the way in which the design would play out in different circumstances: prototyping and serious play
- detailed planning of implementation: support of key power groups, reward desired behaviour, monitor transition
- organizational culture (beliefs and norms) as means and ends
- social learning-loops mechanisms as a way to adapt

[84] David Nadler and Michael Tushman. 1997. *Competing by Design*. Oxford, UK: Oxford University Press.

At the core of this process is the inquiring mind, the designer paying attention to the evolving environment, multiple-looped learning through which ends and means are continually revised as the experiment proceeds: just like the Inuit scraping away at a reindeer antler with his knife, examining it first from this angle and then from another until he cries, "Ah, seal!"[85]

In this inquiry, it has often proved easier to tinker with the technology than with the structure, and easier to tinker with the structure than with the culture of the organization. But it would be unwise to presume that any sequence will always work.

Disclosing new worlds and imparting style

The core task of an inquiring-system design is to disclose new worlds, for organizations are worlds: they are a totality of interrelated pieces of 'equipment' to carry out a specific task (such as hammering in a nail). These tasks are undertaken for some 'purpose' (like building a house); and these activities bestow those accomplishing them with 'identities' (like being a carpenter).[86] This is the sense in which one speaks of the world of medicine, business, or academe – and in which inquiring systems attempt to disclose how these new worlds could and should materialize.

There is more to organizations than the interconnection of equipment, purpose and identities, however. Spinosa et al. use the word 'style' to refer to the ways in which all the practices are coordinated and fit together in an organization. 'Style' is what makes certain kinds of activities and things matter. In a way, 'style' is an echo of culture: it pertains not only to the way coordination is effected, but also to the way transformation is effected.

In their study, Spinosa et al. show how economic, social and political entrepreneurs are those who spot disharmonies between what seem to be the 'rules' in good currency, and what would appear to be the sort of 'practices' likely to be effective.

[85] Donald A. Schön and Martin Rein. 1994. *Frame Reflection – Toward the Resolution of Intractable Policy Controversies*. New York: Basic Books, p. 166-167.
[86] Charles Spinosa, Fernando Flores and Hubert L. Dreyfus. 1997. *Disclosing New Worlds*. Cambridge, MA: MIT Press, p. 17.

They detect anomalies. Those anomalies create puzzles. The reaction to puzzles is often to ignore them and pursue the on-going tasks as usual, instead of recognizing that the anomalies are creating mysteries, and that what is called for are 'ways' of understanding mysteries, the search for "guidelines for solving a mystery by organized exploration of possibilities."[87]

Anomalies trigger reactions from entrepreneurs capable of suggesting alternative ways to retool, restructure, and reframe their activities according to new principles. Their work entails articulating the problem differently, cross-appropriating ways of doing things elsewhere and adjusting them to the task at hand, and reframing the very notion of the business one is in along different lines.

This is the world of prototyping, of experimentation, of serious play. Innovative persons in all areas (economic, political, social) become designers and redefine the style of their organizations.

Phases in the crystallization of the inquiring systems

One can analyze the deployment of a collaborative decentred metagovernance regime as emerging in three phases: (1) the emergence of a focal point for the governance regime; (2) the process through which there is or is not rallying support for it, and through which it acquires legitimacy or not; and (3) the capacity, on the basis of this focal regime, to generate the requisite amount of coordination, resilience, innovation, overcoming and accomplishment. The challenge is to explain how the stewardship emerges without needing to be personalized, and how it generates resilience and high performance – or catastrophe – for there is no guarantee of success.

Emergence

In certain cases, where the situation is relatively simple, a focal point emerges organically. The contextual pressures generate some anomie in the agents. This leads them to search for

---

[87] Roger Martin. 2004. "The Design of Business," *Rotman Magazine*, winter, p. 7.

guideposts, and a focal regime emerges to resolve the tensions among the different points of view. In the case of a pure and perfectly competitive situation, a price system will become the focal regime, as was experienced in the desolate world of POW camps in the 1940s, where the fact that each prisoner received a Red-Cross type standard ration (which did not necessarily match his/her personal pattern of preferences) generated a situation that organically gave rise to generalized trading within the POW camp, with cigarettes used as currency. In a similar way, in a total panic, a crowd movement becomes the reference point. In both cases, coordination emerges without the need for any personalization.

In more complex cases, the collaborative decentred metagovernance regime emerges in more circuitous ways: effective coordination connotes sets of principles, norms, rules, mechanisms and protocols, around which the expectations of agents converge, and around which decision making and implementation get defined. Such a regime may crystallize quickly when the organization is relatively small. Communities of practice 'gel' and, for instance, the board of directors of a small high-tech startup company brings together quite naturally the inventive engineer, the angel financier, the potentially important buyer of the new widget, etc. This forum undertakes the stewarding function.

In yet more complex organizations (private, public, social), the governance regime wears a more formal attire (more legalistic, constraining), and the board is more stylized, but the same logic is at play. In these complex cases, Chait et al. show that the governance regime has a tendency to crystallize in different layers: it is not simply playing the role of financial sentinel (Type I governance), but it also creates a place where the points of view of the different stakeholders get integrated (Type II governance).[88] It is also the locus of discernment, of meaning-making – providing the mental map of the organization, of its environment, its mission, its projects, and proposing the sort

[88] R.P. Chait, W.P. Ryan and B.E. Taylor. 2005. *Governance as Leadership.* Hoboken, NJ: Wiley.

of transformations, innovations and reframing likely to bring the organization beyond its limits into renewal territory (Type III or generative governance). This generative governance unfolds through a robust multilogue, much experimentation, prototyping and social learning, and the collaborative congealing as a community of meaning.

Support and legitimacy

In order for the focal regime built on the inquiring system to be able to resolve all those tensions in a creative way, it must generate a rallying effect that bestows legitimacy. What must emerge is a culture, *une manière de voir,* that establishes the basis of a collective intelligence that facilitates collaboration and underpins collective choices.

How is this collective intelligence constructed? It is through communication and deliberation. A focal regime underwrites a structure, certain rituals and mechanisms that facilitate interactions by stabilizing anticipations. This is the visible face of the metagovernance regime that may trigger either a rallying movement, or a movement of rejection, through the dual logics of synchronicity and destructive cascades.

This movement of contagion may materialize through reasoned discussion and justification, but it may also operate through surprise mechanisms – like modes and fads – via the media that may either dampen the cascade or amplify its impact and generate a movement of polarization. These mechanisms of propagation are relatively poorly understood, and may generate governance regimes that are idiosyncratic, fragile and often surprising.

Only when a metagovernance regime is in place can it be said to be performing well or not. Obviously, the focal regime must make sense of the situation, but, most importantly, it must have a 'great adaptive capacity.'[89] This capacity does not emerge from the 'properties' of the governance regime (that would be usable in all situations and transportable from one situation to another), but from the 'capacities' of a regime that are revealed

---

[89] Warren G. Bennis and R.J. Thomas. 2002. "Crucibles of Leadership," *Harvard Business Review,* 80(9): 39-45.

in situ, in a precise context and particular circumstances. It is the wave that determines if the governance regime as 'surfer' has the required capacities.[90]

Despite the daunting complexity of the emergence and the support phases of the stewardship process, they offer a multiplicity of opportunities for many co-governors to intervene to 'collibrate', and to have an impact on the inquiring system and on the collaborative decentred metagovernance regime.

Effective and creative coordination: uncertain

The principles of good governance that are likely to generate that sort of dynamic adaptive stewardship would have to make good use of the following reference points: inclusion, subsidiarity, multi-stability, and experimentalism. In each case, these reference points must obviously be interpreted, taking into account each particular context, but they cannot be ignored.

Longitude: the inclusion-subsidiarity axis

The first two reference points have to do with the best way to assemble the potential partners when power, resources and information are diffracted, and to structure their coordinated work. The key idea is to include as many of the meaningful stakeholders as possible in the decision-making process (inclusion), and to design the decision-making apparatus in such a way as to allow those closest to the situation to take the decision (subsidiarity). From this ensues the principle of as much decentralization as possible, and only as much centralization as necessary.

Such a participative and distributed governance regime should ensure continuous social learning, quick self-correcting feedback, creative conflict resolution, and the existence of shared responsibility mechanisms in order to generate the right mix of reliability and innovation.

---

[90] Manuel DeLanda. 2006. *A New Philosophy of Society: Assemblage Theory and Social Complexity.* New York: Continuum.

Latitude: the multistability-experimentalism axis

The other two reference points deal with the resolution of tension between exploitation and exploration. The principle of 'multi-stability' is important in the architecture of open systems. It suggests that the best way to fully exploit and to stabilize a differentiated system is to partition it into sub-systems, in order (a) to immunize the system as a whole from the impact of broad shocks that could destabilize it completely, hitting it as a whole; and (b) to be in a position to delegate to a portion of the organization (the one best able to handle the shock) the adjustment job that is appropriate.

But multi-stability also facilitates experimentation, exploration and innovation by allowing them to proceed *par morceaux*. Innovation is creative destruction, and thereby destabilizing. A good governance regime will be fundamentally 'experimentalist,' capable of engaging the organization in new avenues, but safely and prudently – that is, by engaging it tentatively, partially and often *par morceaux*. This form of attentive experimentalism is an essential condition for Type III governance.

*   *   *

Despite the fact that these reference points will help in shaping effective stewardship, there is no assurance that such an outcome will prevail. There are systemic blockages that may prevent such an emergence: an important one being the gridlock fragmentation of ownership powers that may well prevent the assembly of what every stakeholder knows is a winning combination.

There are also acts of sabotage: passive sabotage as a result of neglect, lack of vigilance, sheer incompetence, or active sabotage by powerful vested interests that may see immense benefit for their clan in ensuring that some effective governance regime and stewardship do not materialize.

Perhaps more importantly, ineffective stewardship may evolve because of cognitive dissonance, and a refusal (even in a tentative way) to factor in the dynamic of context and the power of self-organization that are bound to produce surprises (good and bad). These occurrences cannot be ignored, and must be dealt with opportunistically.

The ethical corridor

Collaborative decentred metagoverning is becoming an ongoing conversation within a game without a master, and the new basic unit of analysis is the relationship. These relationships take the form of contracts or conventions that can be more or less formal, and roughly define the legitimate expectations of the partners, and therefore the foundations of both accountability (what is the expected performance) and ethics (what is regarded as acceptable performance).

In order to develop the sort of apparatus likely to be of use in guiding behaviour and choice in such a world, one must be able to build on three guide posts: (a) a good appreciation of context; (b) a sense of the extent to which the organizational culture allows more or less latitude in redefining and reframing issues, in order to ensure goodness of fit with the whole range of potentially contradictory expectations of the partners; and (c) a broad set of reference points that might serve as generic guideposts in defining 'good' behaviour.

It is in the triangulation of these guideposts that one may find ways to navigate safely. It should be explained that 'safety' in ethics amounts to ensuring that decisions are made and action taken in such a manner that (1) all moral contracts are honoured and conventions respected; and (2) all decisions and actions that might violate these norms can be explained in a language that all would find acceptable, if such violations are going to be agreed to.

Critical description is not entirely a matter of individual perception. The cultural environment shapes what one is allowed to perceive. Indeed, the 'sociality' of the organization or of the system defines the way in which issues are framed, and constitutes a set of lenses imposed on the members as a result of their having been somewhat programmed by the social framework within which they are embedded.

In no organization can it be said that all assumptions can be questioned, and all members can allow themselves to tinker with all the mechanisms, structures and principles. Indeed, this is generally the other way around. Most organizations have an 'appreciative system,' and those who do not share it are deviant, outsiders. Moreover, as Warren Bennis put it, "most organizations would rather risk obsolescence than make room for the non-conformist in their midst."[91] Indeed, most institutions are more or less neurotic.

Finally, given a good appreciation of the context and of the sociality (i.e., the constraints and the degrees of freedom that the organization avails to its members in developing strategies within a certain corridor, and the support or non-support for efforts to extend the width of the corridor of acceptable behaviour), it remains but to add the sort of minimal basic norms by reference to which acceptable behaviour might be defined – that is, where the lines in the sand are: the boundaries one should not ignore separating the zones of moral comfort and discomfort.[92]

Since the different parties have different representations of the world, and different frames of reference, the arrangements arrived at may be regarded as 'social armistices' or moral contracts, arrived at by negotiations (explicit or tacit), and purported to be acceptable to most, if not all, parties. They are bound to be flexible and loose enough to be consonant with the different norms and standards of the different groups, and capable of meeting various stringent tests of acceptability before being adopted: reasonableness, fairness, legitimacy, efficiency, etc.

This process is the result of two intertwined sub-processes: the 'emergence of contingent moral contracts' as

[91] Warren G. Bennis. 1976. *The Unconscious Conspiracy.* New York: AMACOM, p. 40.

[92] A benchmark that might serve as a reference is the balancing of the imperatives of the four cardinal virtues: (1) *temperantia* – an awareness and sense of limits; (2) *fortitudo* – a capacity to take into account context and long term; (3) *justitia* – a sense of what is good, and an inclination to search for it; and (4) *prudentia* – a sense of what is practical and reasonable.

a way to make the relationships involved in collaborative decentred metagovernance less intangible, and of 'reflexive' metagovernance, the learning-by-doing and doing-by-learning through which these moral contracts are continually modified, as problem handling and reflection on the whole social learning process reveal the need to do so.

Contingent moral contracts

Collaboration is always contingent: it is built on the tentative premise "I will if you will," and it does not crystallize instantaneously – it develops in stages, sometimes rather painfully, and they may fall apart if circumstances change sufficiently, regardless.[93]

After a period of frustration, when it becomes obvious that one cannot do whatever has to be done alone, and when potential, somewhat-trusted partners are identified, a period of experimentation driven by considerations of costs and benefits becomes possible. In this second stage, building relations and close monitoring are the order of the day; joint action is tentatively experimented with, and trust is strengthened. In the third stage, increased confidence prevails, organizational memory is built, and the possibility of extending the scope of collaboration is envisaged.

The development of loose, flexible and non-enforceable instruments in the nature of the memoranda of understanding of various sorts is a most important way to make tangible and verifiable the process of deepening of trust and confidence, and yet of not killing the budding confidence by demanding very formal contractual arrangements. Whether these take the form of moral contracts or loose conventions, these instruments provide a certain degree of tangibility in a world that remains very elusive.

These modifiable moral contracts serve two major purposes. First, they embody some mechanism of coordination, some basis for defining agreed-upon representations, some ground for justification, and some elements to help shape interpretation

[93] Christopher Wilson. 2007. "Facilitating Contingent Cooperation," *www.optimumonline.ca* 37(1): 1-8.

when some is needed. Second, they serve as a way to anchor, ever so loosely, the basis for monitoring and sanctioning as a foundation for social learning.

In the first case, it should be clear that collaboration cannot be reduced to mechanical coordination devices. Such devices serve well at a first level, but if collaboration is going to evolve smoothly, it must entail the development of some agreement on methods of evaluation and justification for action, and even provide help in interpreting whatever agreement has been arrived at, if and when it becomes necessary.

A whole literature on the economics of conventions has emerged over the last 20 years, and it has shown how such conventions or contingent moral contracts are crucially important in collaboration.[94] This is a new frontier in the development of collaborative decentred metagovernance for it provides the raw material and the intellectual vocabulary necessary to discuss critically the emergence and the design of the network of relationships underpinning successful collaboration.

In the second case, these loose moral contracts provide sufficient precision to allow monitoring and sanctioning to be meaningful. As Howard Rheingold would put it, monitoring and sanctioning are crucial to social learning, and "serve the important function of providing information about others' actions and levels of commitment" – a matter of great importance when it is understood that all collaboration is contingent.[95]

Reflexive governance

However useful moral contracts and conventions might be, they are deliberately elusive and flexible because they will need to serve as guideposts as long as certain circumstances prevail, but may need to evolve as circumstances change. This calls for 'reflexive' governance – governance that has a propensity to self-subversion, that constantly calls into question its own foundations (i.e., its concepts, practices, moral contracts and

[94] Bernard Enjolras. 2006. *Conventions et institutions*. Paris: L'Harmattan.
[95] Howard Rheingold. 2002. *Smart Mobs*. Cambridge, UK: Perseus, p. 176.

conventions), envisions alternatives, and reinvents and reshapes these foundations in the light of changing circumstances and unintended consequences.[96]

This calls not only for multiple-looped learning (i.e., revising not only the means as learning proceeds, but also revising the goals pursued, and even revising the very nature of the game and of the megacommunity involved), but also the emergence of an approach reflecting the interdependencies, understanding the effects of specialized concepts and strategies, and reflecting on the very working of collaborative decentred metagovernance.

Reflexive governance underlines the process of continuous social learning at its core, but requires that the continuous feedback not be restricted to means and ends within a given problem definition, but that reflexivity also triggers problem redefinition as experience is accumulated, and even a reconfiguration of the very approach to governance.

This level of analysis has an autopoïetic quality. It does not pertain only to the process of self-steering, self-regulation, or self-organization, but it aims at disclosing the process of continual self-renewal and self-creation. This general level of analysis would aim at producing a grammar of collaborative governance regimes, in the same way as Elinor Ostrom has been trying to develop a grammar of institutions.[97]

Conclusion

While this characterization of broad-based stewardship in action is significantly different and much more complex than the anthropomorphic cartoons used to represent personalized leadership, simplicity in this case is the source of much unacceptable simplification. In a world where nobody is fully in charge and where there are no common values, the organizations and the social systems can only count on collaborative decentred metagovernance to ensure the requisite social learning, and the desired mix of exploitation and exploration.

[96] Jan-Peter Voß, Dierk Bauknecht and René Kemp (eds.). 2006. *Reflexive Governance for Sustainable Development*. Cheltenham: Edward Elgar, p. 4.
[97] Elinor Ostrom. 2005. *Understanding Institutional Diversity*. Princeton, NJ: Princeton University Press, chapter V.

This entails a better understanding of the ways in which citizens and groups can become co-producers of governance, and of the variety of mechanisms of self-organization, nudging, experimentation and collaboration that can be put to use to ensure social learning, resilience and innovation.

Yet the apparatus built over the last three chapters is unfamiliar enough – and the efforts required to master the new vocabulary, to become appreciative of the new mechanisms, and to take ownership of the new approach are important enough – that one cannot expect that the new cosmology will be adopted easily. This is why we have felt that there was a need to put this new apparatus to use in a number of case studies dealing with various challenges facing inquiring systems, and with various issue domains characterized by particular social learning problems. It is hoped that these case studies of issues of public concern will contribute to reducing the normal unease that accompanies the acquisition of a new language.

Indeed, the additional volumes in the Collaborative Decentred Metagovernance Series should also help to make more obvious the usefulness and the not-so-difficult nature of the task of acquiring this new language of problem definition.

CHAPTER 4

| The New Frontier

Ruth Hubbard and Gilles Paquet

"Fail better."
– Samuel Beckett

Introduction

Public policy often fails. In the regalian world of command-and-control policies of the era of Big 'G' government, these failures were routinely ascribed to external shocks and surprises preventing well-designed policies from nudging complex social systems in preferred directions, without ever really questioning the validity of the policy process as traditionally conceived.

In the new turbulent, more complex, and diverse world of small 'g' governance (in which power, resources, and information are widely distributed, and where nobody is regarded as fully in charge), such *ad hoc* explanations for governance and policy failures are no longer persuasive.[98] Policy appears to fail mostly because of the flaws in the public policy process.

---

[98] Gilles Paquet. 1999. "Innovations in Governance in Canada," *Optimum*, 29(2-3): 71-81 (see www.optimumonline.ca /archives).

These flaws are the unrealistic assumptions of the 'goal-setting and control' view of public policy about (1) public policy makers being informed enough to elicit clear goals and stable means-ends relationships (when policy issues pose 'wicked problems');[99] (2) governing being a top-down process (when it is of necessity more and more horizontal and collaborative); and (3) the requisite amount of collaboration for effective public policy being either inconsequential or materializing organically, if and when required (when it is blatantly not the case). As a result, the public policy process mostly fails because the *problématique* is flawed: it is based on grossly incomplete basic information, simplistically sketched models, and the challenge of ensuring the requisite collaboration is irresponsibly occluded.[100]

Except in trivial circumstances, the public policy process is, at best, a matter of trial-and-error that must routinely fail, and a prudent attitude calls for action *ab ovo* to put in place a robust and quickly adaptive social

---

[99] Wicked policy problems have two major characteristics: the goals are not known or are very ambiguous, and the means-ends relationships are highly uncertain and poorly understood (Horst W.J. Rittel and Melvin M. Webber. 1973. "Dilemmas in a General Theory of Planning," *Policy Sciences*, 4(2): 155-169; Gilles Paquet. 1999. *Governance Through Social Learning*. Ottawa: University of Ottawa Press, chapter 2).

[100] There have been many attempts in the past to free the public policy framework from these strictures. The works of Harold Wilensky, Geoffrey Vickers, Charles Lindblom, Amitai Etzioni and many others have provided a much more realistic view of the policy process. But the shadow of 'policy science' with its goal-and-control focus has remained omnipresent in policy discussions, especially with the new focus on marksmanship and quantophrenia in policy analysis, in economics but also elsewhere. Gilles Paquet. 2009. *Scheming virtuously: the road to collaborative governance*. Ottawa: Invenire Books, chapter 1; Ruth Hubbard and Gilles Paquet. 2010. *The Black Hole of Public Administration*. Ottawa: University of Ottawa Press, chapter 4.

learning apparatus, and the requisite 'fail-safe' and 'safe-fail' mechanisms.[101]

Given the ever greater complexity and wickedness of policy arenas, the greater importance and extent of the megacommunities[102] that need to be actively or passively involved in collaboration for the policies to succeed, and the faster pace of change that requires almost continuous adjustments, the focus of the public policy process has to be shifted from goals and controls to intelligence and innovation.[103] The public policy process has to be redefined as an 'inquiring system,'[104] adapting constantly through serious play[105] with prototypes,[106] and equipped with as many self-correcting, learning, transformative and 'new-direction-seeking' mechanisms as possible, since error and failure correction is likely to be the name of the game.[107]

---

[101] 'Fail-safe' mechanisms are simple, normal add-on precautionary measures that due diligence calls for when a relatively safe process may be derailed on occasion. 'Safe-fail' mechanisms are essential measures that are called for as part of the core policy design because it is assumed that the process is most likely to fail as a result of the very dynamics of organizations that evolve in cycles of exploitation of resources, containment, creative destruction and renewal (C.S (Buzz) Holling and Lance H. Gunderson. 2002. "Resiliency and Adaptive Cycles" in L.H. Gunderson and C.S. Holling, (eds). *Panarchy: Understanding Transformations in Human and Natural Systems*. London, UK: Island Press, p. 25-62).

[102] Mark Gerencser et al. 2008. *Megacommunities*. New York: Palgrave Macmillan.

[103] Harold L. Wilensky. 1967. *Organizational Intelligence*. New York: Basic Books; Gilles Paquet. 2009. *Scheming virtuously: the road to collaborative governance*, chapter 1.

[104] C. West Churchman. 1971. *The Design of Inquiring Systems*. New York: Basic Books.

[105] Michael Schrage. 2000. *Serious Play*. Boston: Harvard Business School Press.

[106] Alicia Juarreno. 2010. "Complex Dynamical Systems Theory," www.cognitive-edge.com; C.S. (Buzz) Holling. 1976. "Resilience and Stability of Ecosystems" in Eric Jantsch and C.H. Waddington, (eds). *Evolution and Consciousness in Transition*. Reading, MA.: Addison-Wesley, p. 73-92.

[107] This is in no way the same as attempts to redefine the goal-and-control model as operating through circuitous and oblique ways while remaining in a goal-and-control mode *stricto sensu* (John Kay. 2011. *Obliquity – Why our goals are best achieved indirectly*. New York: The Penguin Press).

In this chapter, we probe first the foundations on which the public policy process as an inquiring system can be built, and why, in this approach, 'safe-fail' mechanisms are so crucially important, given the eco-cyclical dynamics of organizations. Secondly, we discuss very briefly the challenges of two broad policy issues (health, and productivity and innovation) show evidence of flagrant policy failures; argue that failures can be ascribed, to a significant extent, to the flaws of the traditional public policy process; and suggest that the reframed public policy process as 'inquiring-system-cum-safe-fail' mechanisms, inspired by collaborative decentred metagovernance, might indicate ways forward in these two issue domains.

Inquiring systems, social learning and safe-fail mechanisms

Inquiring systems are processes that ensure improvement in ongoing and transformative cross-sectional and inter-temporal coordination (when power, resources and information are widely distributed) through the operations of an ever improving kind of 'automatic pilot' (if one can use this metaphor) in order to allow the organization or the socio-technical system not only to operate effectively, efficiently and productively at any point in time, but also to adapt innovatively to new circumstances, and to transform itself accordingly as this becomes necessary.

The automatic pilot is a nexus of adjustment mechanisms that is constantly updated as the inquiring system acquires good and bad experiences that suggest modifications in the adjustment mechanisms. Thus, much of the 'wayfinding' is the result of the vegetative or reactive functions of the automatic pilot, but there is also a constant need for refurbishment of the governance process. An inquiring system may emerge not only from self-organization, and may require active redesign intervention as a result of the new social learning.

There are common questions facing the designers of inquiring systems at all levels. How does the automatic pilot (as a nexus of adjustment mechanisms) define what is the problem? What are the non-negotiable constraints in the megacommunity? What is the task at hand? Who are the stakeholders that cannot be ignored if the system is to be nudged collaboratively? What can be done to mobilize the support of collaborators? What instruments might be used, and conventions or moral contracts negotiated, to maintain the active commitment of members to the partnership? What about the shared value-adding expected and the evaluation mechanisms required? And how does it ensure that the learning loops necessary for social learning proceed aptly and that the 'fail-safe' mechanisms are in place and modified as necessary? Most importantly, since it is presumed that this inquiring system is likely to fail often, it is crucial to design *ab ovo* the 'safe-fail' mechanisms for the system to cope effectively with extreme failures, and to have in place the required capacities and competencies to transform, so that the organization can emerge renewed and not destroyed from 'creative destruction' experiences.

Emerging wayfinding

The shift from goal-setting and control to intelligence and innovation means that policy is no longer a bow-arrow-target game. An inquiring system is a pro-active search and exploration process fuelling social learning. The likelihood that experiments will fail is ascribable to the fact that the socio-economic system to be nudged is so complex, and the art of public strategy-making is so imperfect.[108]

The new approach to public policy in terms of intelligence and innovation delves much more deeply into the workings of issue domains. Intelligence refers to the problem of gathering, processing, interpreting and communicating the technical and political information and knowledge needed for a modicum of effectiveness in the decision-making processes. Innovation is tinkering with the system at the meso and micro levels – for

---

[108] Geoff Mulgan. 2009. *The Art of Public Strategy.* Oxford, UK: Oxford University Press.

this is where the rubber hits the road – through modification of the collective intelligence of the communities of practice.[109]

The new public policy process as inquiring system proceeds in ways that are in keeping with the megacommunity,[110] gropes with the mission of shared value-adding that is pursued,[111] and appreciates the challenges of mobilizing the required collaborative and catalyzing learning loops to ensure quick reactions to dysfunctions, as well as develops the competencies required for self-transformation.

Whatever stewardship emerges is not entirely the result of a deliberate strategy, but in the nature of 'emerging wayfinding,' is due to a variety of gestures and actions by partners (as the experience unfolds), with the result that additional knowledge accrues and triggers yet more gestures and actions. Public policy is not mainly about managing resources to some advantage as gauged by an objective function (even though it has been reduced to this by managers as a matter of convenience), but about "attaining and sustaining a set of organized relationships nested within wider systems in order to experience the possibility of doing things differently and, potentially, better."[112]

Figure 5 captures the ambit that the process has to span.

---

[109] Communities of practice are the relevant units that both can learn and transform as they learn (Étienne Wenger. 1998. *Communities of Practice.* Cambridge, UK: Cambridge University Press). For an exploration of the processes underpinning the re-arrangements of the governance model as social learning proceeds, see Gilles Paquet, 2009, *Scheming virtuously: the road to collaborative governance,* chapters 2 and 5.

[110] "A megacommunity is any large ongoing sphere of interest where governments, corporations, NGOs and others intersect over time. The participants remain interdependent because their common interest compels them to work together, even though they might not see, describe, or approach their mutual problem or situation in the same way." Mark Gerencser et al. 2008. *Megacommunities.* New York: Palgrave Macmillan, p. 54.

[111] Michael E. Porter and Mark R. Kramer. 2011, "The Big Idea: Creating Shared Value," *Harvard Business Review,* 89(1-2): 62-77.

[112] Robert C.H. Chia and Robin Holt. 2009. *Strategy without Design – The silent efficacy of indirect action.* Cambridge, UK: Cambridge University Press, p. ix, 112.

FIGURE 5.
X-ray of the Public Policy Process as Inquiring System

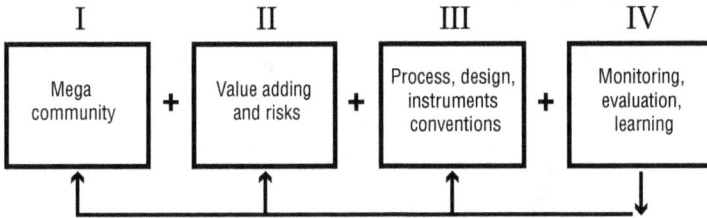

I		II		III		IV
Mega community	+	Value adding and risks	+	Process, design, instruments conventions	+	Monitoring, evaluation, learning

What may not transpire from such a depiction is the extent to which, in a small 'g' governance world, engagement with the environment and the partners entails "local adaptations and ingenuity in everyday practical coping ... acting purposively to deal with immediate concerns at hand but doing so in habituated ways ...." Wayfinding is "reaching out into the unknown and developing an incomplete but practically sufficient comprehension of the situation in order to cope effectively with it. Prospective rather than retrospective sense-making is involved ... [and wayfinding] is continuously clarified through each iterative action and adjustment and not through any predetermined agenda."[113]

Social learning α: cognitive and information diffusion level

An inquiring system has no safe and assured pathway ahead. It is a proactive probing and exploration system that is on the lookout for anomalies, their sources and causes, for cumulatively clarified problem definition, for the identification of who needs to be involved in dealing with the issue, for ways in which micro-reactions might be cast in more general contexts, for groping instruments as well as for alliances and moral contracts with other parties that might help in the process, and finally, for anything that might help in accelerating the process of social learning and experimentation and opening new vistas. The success of the operation should be gauged

[113] Robert C.H. Chia and Robin Holt, 2009, p. 159.

not so much by reference to myopic measurable temporary outcomes (that may often be quite misleading), but mainly by the modification of habits and belief systems, and by the effectiveness of the mechanisms in place to modify the very nature of the game, if and when the inquiring system gives signs of being derailed or of being guided out of the corridor defined by acceptable norms.[114]

In an effort to help identify the major obstacles to social learning (and therefore to guide the process of intervention), Max Boisot has suggested a simple mapping of the social learning cycle in a three-dimensional space – 'the information space' – which maps the degree of 'abstraction', 'codification', and 'diffusion' of the information flows within organizations: the farther away from the origin on the vertical axis, the more the information is codified (i.e., the more its form is clarified, stylized and simplified); the farther away from the origin laterally eastward, the more widely the information is diffused and shared; and the farther away from the origin laterally westward, the more abstract the information is (i.e., the more general the categories in use).

The social learning cycle in Figure 6 may be decomposed into two phases, with three steps in each phase: phase I emphasizes the cognitive dimensions of the cycle; phase II the diffusion of the new information.

In phase I, learning begins with some scanning of the environment in order to detect anomalies and paradoxes. Following this first step (s), one is led to step 2 to stylize the problem (p), posed by the anomalies and paradoxes, in a language of problem solution; the third step of phase I purports to generalize the solution found to the more specific issue to a broader family of problems, through a process of abstraction (at). In phase II, the new knowledge is diffused (d) to a larger community of persons or groups in step 4; then there is a process of absorption (ar) of this new knowledge by the population

---

[114] Max H. Boisot. 1995. *Information Space*. London: Routledge; Gilles Paquet, 2009, *Scheming virtuously: the road to collaborative governance*, chapter 5.

so as to become part of the tacit stock of knowledge in step 5; in step 6, the new knowledge is not only absorbed, but has an impact (i) on the concrete practices of the group or community.

Figure 6 allows us to identify the different potential blockages through the learning cycle. In Phase I, cognitive dissonance in (s) may prevent the anomalies from being noted, inhibitions of all sorts in (p) may stop the process of translation into a language of problem solution, and blockages (at) may keep the new knowledge from acquiring the most effective degree of generality. In Phase II, the new knowledge may not get the appropriate diffusion because of property rights (d), or because of the strong dynamic conservatism which may generate a refusal to listen by those most likely to profit from the new knowledge (ar), or because of difficulties in finding ways to incorporate the new knowledge (i).

FIGURE 6. **Learning Cycle and Potential Blockages**

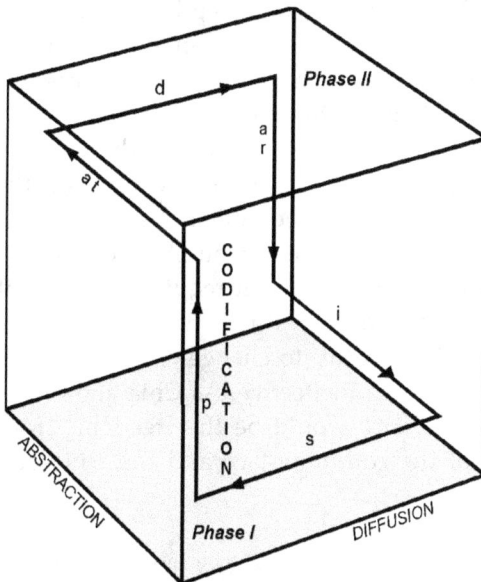

Source: Max Boisot. 1995. Information Space. London: Routledge, p. 190.

Figure 6 may be interpreted as making possible a checklist of potential sources of blockages or failures in the inquiring system. Interventions to remove or attenuate the learning blockages always entail some degree of interference with the mechanisms of collective intelligence, relational transactions, and therefore the psycho-social fabric of the organization.[115]

Social learning β : collaborative process level

A crucial component of this inquiring system is collaboration. If power, resources and information are widely distributed among many hands and heads, no effective 'wayfinding' can emerge without collaboration. Yet participants are different; they are invited to stay connected and to engage with persons with different belief systems. This cannot be accomplished without some modicum of trust, sharing, belonging and respect in this co-creation process, even though the only truly shared sentiment to begin with is discomfort with the *status quo*.[116]

Collaboration entails recognizing that one cannot do it alone, that one must take a step beyond individual needs "to call forth possibilities from an unknown and not-yet-possible future," and such a courage to collaborate translates into a way of being. This will be instituted in a variety of conventions: some explicit and legal, others tacit and quasi-emotional. Collaboration is meant to broaden the problem definition and to widen the potential responses to problems that emerge from silo-thinking, but it is never clear that these possibilities will materialize. It requires the capacity to keep going and to endure when things do not look promising, and to maintain the capacity to change course when the original arrangement proves ineffective. As Chia and Holt would put it, the right balance would be the freedom "from both the obstinacy of the commonplace and the iridescent glare of the new."[117]

---

[115] Gilles Paquet. 2001. "Collective Intelligence," *Lac Carling Governments' Review*, (June-July): 28-29.

[116] Alycia Lee and Tatiana Glad. 2011. *Collaboration: the courage to step into a meaningful mess.* Spokane, WA: Berkana Institute.

[117] Robert C.H. Chia and Robin Holt, 2009, p. 212.

The ecology of the inquiring system at work entails a cycle of social learning in four phases that might be regarded as the standard learning process in normal times – with an 'observation and cognitive' phase, an 'investigative' phase, a 'design-cum-moral contracts' phase, and an 'evaluative and social learning' phase, as explained in chapter 2.[118]

Since most policies are likely to fail, the inquiring system has to be equipped with the requisite mechanisms to ensure that the system can minimize the costs of failure: routine 'fail-safe' mechanisms (FSM) aiming at ensuring resilience, that is, keeping the organization within a corridor constrained by certain bounds in normal times.

The FSM may be simply formulated in terms of resilience or sustainability, *à la* Geoffrey Vickers,[119] or in the form of basic conditions for the public policy to be acceptable, *à la* Carl Taylor (a test to determine if what is proposed is technically feasible, socially acceptable, implementable, and not too politically destabilizing).[120]

Social learning γ : dynamic organizational level

Organizations and systems are also periodically hit by shocks that threaten the very existence of the original setting. A set of essential variables is affected, and it triggers step-mechanisms that command fundamental transformations if the system is to survive. 'Safe-fail' mechanisms (SFM) are not routine mechanisms aimed at resilience, they are meant to trigger dramatic transformation, when the organization is faced with dramatic forms of creative destruction – experiences that command trans-substantiation and self-reinvention as the only way to survive.

Buzz Holling and other experts have suggested that both natural and human organizations go through somewhat periodic eco-cycles of the sort sketched in Figure 7.

---

[118] Gilles Paquet and Christopher Wilson. 2011. "Collaborative Co-Governance as Inquiring Systems," *www.optimumonline.ca*, 41(2) : 1-12.

[119] Geoffrey Vickers. 1965. *The Art of Judgment*. London, UK: Chapman & Hall.

[120] These questions are derived from a general framework developed by Carl Taylor. 1997. "The ACIDD Test: a framework for policy planning and decision making," *Optimum*, 27(4) : 53-62.

FIGURE 7. The Organizational Ecocycle

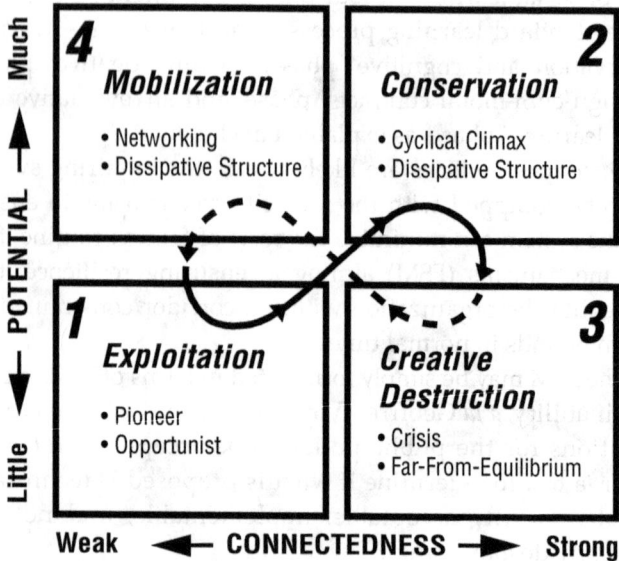

Adapted from C.S. (Buzz) Holling. 1987. "Simplifying the Complex: The paradigms of ecological function and structure," European Journal of Operational Research (30): 139-146; and David K. Hurst and Brenda J. Zimmerman. 1994. "From Life Cycle to Ecocycle: A New Perspective on the Growth, Maturity, Destruction and Renewal of Complex Systems," Journal of Management Inquiry, 3(4): 349.

According to this view, organizations move from situations of exploitation of existing resources (Phase 1: low potential, loose connectedness, entrepreneurial) to moments when more tightly connected forms of organization (institutionalized and more strongly connected in order to fully take advantage of a higher potential) bump into constraints due to the very rigidities brought forth by institutionalization (Phase 2: bureaucratization, rigidity). This leads to vulnerability, to changes that can be a threat to inflexible organizations facing Schumpeterian shocks and crises created by innovations as a result of environmental pressures or technical breakthroughs (Phase 3: crisis, fragmentation). Then, either the organization cannot cope (with the result that it disappears or is dramatically wounded), or it reacts by renewal that mobilizes resources in new configurations, often much more loosely connected, as a result of creative tension (Phase 4: diverse paths to renewal, high potential, weak connectedness). The cycle starts again as this new potential gets diffused in start-ups and projects of diverse sorts.[121]

SFMs create something tantamount to a 'state of exception' that temporarily suspends the normal course of affairs, and play a key role in the transition from Phase 3 to Phase 4, to prevent crucial loss of potential and, perhaps, implosion.

In order to be effective, SFMs require an early warning system, capable of detecting the existence of 'black swan phenomena': either some 'observatory' charged with intelligent environmental scanning, or particular moments when mission reviews are mandated. Required as well are forums for deliberation and negotiation, capable of (1) providing a refinement of the problem definition; (2) suggesting ways in which improved collaboration might be generated; and (3) proposing mechanisms through which newly discovered impediments to such collaboration might be neutralized. Finally, there must be a real possibility of 'experimentation' on the road to renewal in full awareness of the tentative nature of the experiments.[122]

Such mechanisms need not necessarily result in explicit, drastic, glorious revolutions. Often, in environments crippled with a culture of entitlements and powerful mental prisons, draconian moves can only lead to confrontations from which little can emerge but stalemates. As a result, much change occurs

---

[121] C.S. (Buzz) Holling. 1987. "Simplifying the Complex: The paradigms of ecological function and structure," *European Journal of Operational Research*, (30): 139-146; David K. Hurst and Brenda J. Zimmerman. 1994. "From Life Cycle to Ecocycle: A New Perspective on the Growth, Maturity, Destruction and Renewal of Complex Systems," *Journal of Management Inquiry*, 3(4): 339-354.

[122] A general approach has been sketched in Ruth Hubbard and Gilles Paquet. 2006. "Réinventer notre architecture institutionnelle," *Policy Options* 27(7): 57-64; Joseph McCann, John Selsky and James Lee. 2009. "Building Agility, Resilience and Performance in Turbulent Environments," *People & Strategy*, 32(3): 44-51.

underground, *petit à petit*, with as little controversial public discussion as possible, but not necessarily in a less effective way – to the despair of those obsessed by the need for explicit deliberation theatrics.

Healthcare

Canada's universal public healthcare insurance system for hospital and 'necessary' physician services (governed by the 1984 *Canada Health Act* (CHA)) is currently seen by half of the Canadian population as requiring fundamental reform.[123]

The CHA-governed system generates steep cost increases (circa 8 percent per year – at a pace higher than the growth of the GDP),[124] quality that is patchy and not comparatively much good overall, and a mode of production that is not efficient. International comparisons show that, based on the most-recent data, Canada ranks 10th out of 16 peer countries in terms of getting what she pays for in healthcare. Despite Canada's spending being the second highest, it ranked dead last for timeliness and overall quality, and second to last on efficiency.[125]

The cost increases have been declared essentially unsustainable.[126] Yet this under-performing system absorbs an ever-larger portion of provincial/territorial budgets, extinguishes the possibility of addressing other key issues, forces the rationing of specialized service and the de-listing of some services covered, and makes some desirable expansions of the system, on which all agree, simply unaffordable.

[123] Health Council of Canada. 2010. "How do Canadians Rate the Health Care System? Results from the 2010 Commonwealth Fund International Health Policy Survey", *Canadian Health Care Matters'*, Bulletin 4 (November).

[124] See Brett J. Skinner and Mark Rovere. 2011. "Canada's Medicare Bubble: Is Government Health Spending Sustainable Without User-based Funding," Fraser Institute, 'Studies in Health Care', April.

[125] See "Mirror, Mirror on the Wall," *Commonwealth Fund*, 2010 Update.

[126] David A. Dodge and Richard Dion. 2011. "Chronic Healthcare Spending Disease: A Macro Diagnosis and Prognosis," *C.D. Howe Institute Commentary*, (327) April.

Problems

The goal-and-control approach has led to an obsession about certain quantitative indicators (like wait time, or the percentage of public sector budgets going to healthcare), and has often allowed these guideposts to become policy targets, while leaving the flawed healthcare system undisturbed. In fact, the major force behind the growth in health expenditures is not necessarily or mainly abuses of the system, (although they bear a portion of the blame) or the aging of the population, or the like. The main factor behind this increase in demand, according to some experts, is the fact that the income elasticity of demand for healthcare in advanced countries is quite high: as family income rises by 1 percent, healthcare consumption rises by 1.6 percent.[127]

As a result of this craving for healthcare, innovations and productivity gains which reduce the cost and the intrusiveness of certain procedures may not necessarily reduce expenditures on healthcare. They reduce the unit cost and price of the procedure, and, as a result, demand increases as price goes down. Consequently total health expenditures increase further.

This dynamic cannot be tamed with superficial interventions, focusing on symptoms. One must focus on the causes and sources of the dysfunction, and on experiments with plausible mechanisms to correct them, as well as to adapt to evolving circumstances.[128] The challenge is to find ways to control costs, while expanding patient access, and improving care quality. The broad objective is to eliminate what has been

[127] Based on 120 years of data by Robert W. Fogel, co-holder of the 1993 Nobel prize in Economics, from his book *The Fourth Great Awakening and the Future of Egalitarianism*, Chicago: The University of Chicago Press, 2000 (quoted in Gérard Bélanger. 2011. "Faut-il dénoncer le gouffre des dépenses des soins de santé?" *www.optimumonline*, 41(4): 57-68). Bélanger argues persuasively that this sort of growth in demand for healthcare is quite normal, and that the alarmist writings on the unsustainability of the growth of public healthcare expenditures has little to do with abnormal growth in demand, but much to do with the demand being prevented from finding its supply by artificial impediments.

[128] Jens Ludwig et al. 2011. "Mechanism Experiments and Policy Evaluations," *Journal of Economic Perspectives*, 25(3): 17-38.

estimated as a 30-40 percent waste of the total healthcare spending that is ascribable to systemic underuse, overuse and misuse as a result of coordination failures.[129] While these estimates have been made for the United States, there is no reason to believe that the same waste due to coordination failures does not apply to Canada.

Why such failure?

The problem with the existing CHA regime is coordination failures at many levels: among providers, between payers and patients, but also within the healthcare production system *per se*.

The CHA regime has mandated that there should be a public monopoly on the supply of basic health services. This prevents citizens from obtaining services elsewhere. The difficulty, therefore, does not reside in the demand for healthcare services, but with (1) a CHA that prevents the demand from being satisfied by other private/not-for-profit providers, paid for by private citizens; (2) the assumption that citizens have a sacred right to receive basic healthcare services free from the public sector monopoly; (3) the immense power of corporatist groups that prevents the modification of the production process; and (4) a general failure of accountability in the whole system.[130]

As a result, governments are faced with citizens who wish to pay the lowest possible taxes, and providers who act as if their services were costless and who have little acknowledgement of the central importance of collaboration among them. The state can only respond to the demands of both consumers and providers by increasing the resources available for this sector – which will yield very little improvement and must, at the same time, reduce expenditures accordingly in less electorally-

---

[129] Joyit S. Choudhury et al. 2011. "Transforming Healthcare Delivery," *strategy + business*, (64): 5p.

[130] Douglas E. Angus and Monique Bégin. 1999. "Governance in Health Care: Dysfunctions and Challenges," *Transactions of the Royal Society of Canada*, series VI, volume X, p. 171-193.

sensitive issue domains, like infrastructure.[131] Corporatist health professionals obviously want to protect their turf in the current system, and this stands in the way of necessary collaboration and potential innovations that could generate real improvements.[132] In addition, there is little political taste to restrain too firmly unionized healthcare professionals (who can take the population hostage) in the name of optimization of production and service delivery.[133]

The way out

The inquiring system likely to refurbish the healthcare system needs to repair the coordination failures, and this cannot be accomplished without a myriad of changes to the incentive reward systems, the collaboration of providers, better use of standardized proven and effective care protocols, and more engagement of patients in their own care. At the core of these changes are two major challenges: (1) to rebuild responsibility and accountability relations within the healthcare system (in order to contain, among other things, the population's sense of unlimited entitlements to free services from the public sector); and (2) to transform the structure

[131] This is hardly surprising. The dynamics of federal-provincial relations has led to massive unconditional transfers from the federal government to the provincial governments over the last decade. The more organized groups (the healthcare professionals) have been best able to capture this additional money without generating much improvement to the healthcare system. The salary of physicians has doubled over the last decade (Karen Howlett. 2011. "Doctors' ranks and salaries are on the rise," *Globe & Mail* (December 16): A9.

[132] Sholom Glouberman and Henry Mintzberg. 2001. "Managing the Care of Health and the Cure of Disease – Part I: Differentiation" and "Managing the Care of Health and the Cure of Disease – Part II: Integration," *Health Care Management Review*, 26(1) 56-69 and 70-84, respectively.

[133] It was not especially wise for the federal government to put a blank cheque for federal transfers to the provinces on the table for a decade (*à la* Paul Martin) since it could only be regarded as an invitation for the most organized groups of healthcare personnel to put pressure on the provincial governments to increase their salaries. This is exactly what has happened in the last decade (Karen Howlett, 2011, A9).

and functioning of the healthcare system by injecting into it the requisite amount of competition necessary to stimulate innovation and continuous productivity gains.

On the first front, experts are clear. Even if there were unprecedented efficiency and effectiveness improvements, Canadians "face difficult but necessary choices as to how we finance the rising costs of healthcare and manage the rising share of additional income devoted to it."[134] This is not only inevitable, but urgent.

This calls for an acceptance that consumers must shoulder a greater portion of the financial burden of healthcare by various forms of co-payments (something which has recently occurred innocuously, in the form of governments delisting services, or by ingenious circumventions of the CHA rules).[135] In addition, there must be an acceptance of new collaborative relations among governments and with other stakeholders (including the private sector).

The World Health Organization has shown that the French healthcare system (with user fees for most services, and with a significant portion of the hospitals in private hands) has been ranked as the best healthcare system in the world. There is no reason to believe that, if the existence of user fees on most services, and the cohabitation of public and private providers have been accepted widely in France, they could not, if properly explained, be found acceptable in Canada – where, for the moment, these issues are taboo topics.

What will prepare Canadians to accept these new realities is the clear message that a transformation (as a result of a

---

[134] David A. Dodge and Richard Dion, 2011, p. 11.

[135] Some call for a new explicit moral contract that normalizes this process, but what is more likely is a slow, surreptitious and irreversible transformation being carried on by citizens, through the constraints of the CHA being enforced less and less to the point of it becoming irrelevant and not just obsolete. Vandna Bhatia. 2011. "Health Care Spending and the Politics of Drift," in Christopher Stoney and G. Bruce Doern, (eds). *How Ottawa Spends 2011-12 – Trimming Fat or Slicing Pork?* Montreal: McGill-Queen's University Press, p. 180-197.

Schumpeterian shock) is essential if Medicare is to survive. This message that there are limits to the proportion of public spending to be devoted to healthcare if governments are to attend to other needs of Canadians has been heard, but has not been understood or accepted. It will require a brutal awakening via a massive delisting of covered services to break the hold of the culture of entitlements, and to lead Canadians to face the fact that they will need to use complementary private insurance for the growing segment of healthcare services that will not be covered in the future by the 'basic protection' provided by the state.[136]

The second front would entail collaborative care delivery approaches to redesign the production system of healthcare. It cannot be done globally. Experiments should be carried out at the meso-level through pilot projects that can show what will and will not work.[137] This would entail both a new division of labour among health professionals and with other partners, and the redesign of healthcare organizations as a result of these experiments.

To accelerate social learning on this front, it is imperative to relax the existing constraints on experimentation imposed by corporatist groups. This would encourage various communities to launch alternative ways to deliver the full range of their healthcare, in the way the Sault Saint Marie and Algoma District Group Health Centre (SSM) – an acknowledged poster child for effective alternate ways to

[136] One recent poll found that two out of three Canadians would accept a change that allowed them to buy private insurance in non-publicly funded facilities (Kate Allen. 2010. "Canadians warm up to medical user fees: poll," *Globe and Mail* (June 7): A2). Quebec tried to introduce a $25 fee for medical appointments, but backtracked a few months later saying the province wasn't ready for it. On the challenge of having to find ways out of the present financial conumdrum, see David A. Dodge and Richard Dion, 2011.

[137] Amy C. Edmondson. 2011. "Strategies for Learning from Failures," *Harvard Business Review*, 89(4): 48-55; for a succinct review of ongoing experiments in the U.S. (accountable care organizations, patient-centered medical homes, etc.), see Joyit S. Choudhury et al, 2011.

organize the healthcare system – have done. This arrangement is the result of collaboration between a community not-for-profit organization and an independent quality health medical group that by 2010 was providing primary care to 80 percent (some 62,000 persons) of the patients in the area. Since 1963 (when it was spearheaded by locals of the United Steelworkers of America),[138] it has thrived, despite systematic active obstruction from both government and corporatist groups.[139]

Given the difficulties in initiating the always difficult conversations on these topics, in the face of both deeply ingrained mental prisons and immense financial considerations at stake for health professionals and other stakeholders, the only way to ensure that such issues are going to be raised regularly is to decree – as a 'safe-fail' mechanism – that such legal frameworks as the CHA should (like the *Bank Act*) be statutorily reviewed in depth every 10 years.

A looming decennial review would encourage experiments, and pilot or demonstration projects, in preparation for crucial moments when reforms would have to be considered openly. The evolution of banking regulations to keep abreast of transformations in the environment has shown that this decennial review, while not a panacea, has provided a momentum for action and a source of political courage. It might also provide a forum that would contribute to eroding, ever so slightly, the culture of entitlements and the mental prisons in

---

[138] Its early history and struggles are documented in Jonathan Lomas. 1985. *First and Foremost in Community Health Centre*. Toronto: University of Toronto Press.

[139] Although in 1975 health services organizations (Health Service Organizations (HSOs) of which SSM is one) were considered as experimental pilots and then touted as "part of mainstream healthcare services" by the then health minister in 1982, in 1990 the Ministry of Health issued a moratorium on development and applications for HSOs. SSM's mid-80s evaluation was described as "hampered by medical and governmental attitudes as well as difficulties in attempting to compare fee-for-service payment with more of a capitation process." Review by W.B. Spaulding of the Jonathan Lomas, 1985 book cited in the preceeding note, http://www.cbmh.ca/index.php/cbmh/article/viewFile/155/154 [accessed July 27, 2011].

good currency. Such moments of review might even accelerate somewhat the subterranean process of adjustment in the inter-decanal period, because the canonical act would no longer be perceived as non-negotiable.[140]

Productivity and innovation

Since the middle 1990s, Canada's performance on the productivity and innovation fronts has been very weak, as compared to the other OECD countries. Indeed, it has been problematic since the early 1970s. Andrew Sharpe has documented this "abysmal" counter performance on the productivity front in a large number of studies at the Centre for the Study of Living Standards.[141] With regard to innovation, the Conference Board of Canada has rated Canada's performance

[140] The next occasion for introducing such a 'safe-fail' mechanism and to ensure it is robustly put in operation is the expiration of the *Canada Health Accord* in 2014. Instead of continuing to transfer financial resources to the provinces to perpetuate a system that everyone agrees is costing a lot and not delivering value for money, this might be an occasion to reform healthcare in a way that is similar to the reform of welfare in the 1990s. In that case, it led to a reduction of the welfare dependency rate (the percentage of the population on welfare) from 10.7% in 1994 to 5.1% in 2009. This would require that the Canada Health Transfer be reduced and certainly not increased, that the federal government allow the provinces the maximum amount of flexibility to design, regulate and provide healthcare to citizens, and that the *Canada Health Act* be amended to provide the provinces with the requisite amount of flexibility, and to facilitate innovation and experimentation. A prototype of what might be done along these lines has been sketched by Jason Clemens. 2011. *Reforming the Canada Health Transfer*. Ottawa: The Macdonald-Cartier Institute, October.

[141] Andrew Sharpe. 2007. *Three Policies to Improve Productivity Growth in Canada*. CSLS Research Report 2007-45, December; Andrew Sharpe. 2010. *Unbundling Canada's Weak Productivity Performance: The Way Forward*. CSLS Research Report, February; Andrew Sharpe and Eric Thompson. 2010. "Insights into Canada's Abysmal Post 2000 Productivity Performance from Decompositions of Labour Productivity Growth by Industry and Province," *International Productivity Monitor*, 20 (Fall): 48-67. In the 1947-73 period, when productivity grew at 4% per year, the standard of living would double every 18 years or so; in the last while, productivity has grown at less than 1%, and, as a result, one would expect the standard of living to double only every 70 years, that is, three to four times more slowly.

since the 1980s at D (i.e., 14th out of the 17 industrialized countries it examined for its 2009 report card on Canada).[142]

The factors behind this poor productivity and innovation performance are still badly understood. This has not stopped activist governments from boldly proposing policy schemes on the basis of putative linkages between variables they thought they could control, and outcomes judged desirable.

Problems

Despite public support, and some of the most generous tax credits for R&D in the world, business expenditures on R&D as a percentage of GDP remain much lower than in the other G-8 countries, and is declining.[143] Much of the failure to keep up with the other industrialized countries on the productivity and innovation fronts can be ascribed to a poor appreciation of the dynamics of productivity and innovation, and an inadequate characterization of the Canadian socio-economy.

First, productivity increase and innovation emerge not from those exercises in marksmanship by government on the basis of the partial knowledge of planners, but from competitive pressures on the socio-economy's enterprises and concerns to ensure that, as a matter of survival, (1) they produce a better new mousetrap, or a better way to produce the old mousetrap; (2) they generate some routinization of the innovation process that allows an escape from the dependency on fortunate happenstance to find better ways; and (3) they disseminate new proprietary technology voluntarily, even to competitors.[144]

Canada has deliberately reduced this pressure by a policy of limiting competition. For instance, Bell, Rogers, and Telus have been allowed to dominate the wireless market in Canada, and the Canadian government has retained significant restrictions to foreign investment in the telecom sector. This has resulted

---

[142] The Conference Board of Canada. 2009. *How Canada Performs – A Report Card on Canada*. Ottawa: The Conference Board of Canada.

[143] Kevin Lynch. 2011. "Productivity and Innovation: Competing to Win," *Policy Options*, 32(4): 52-56.

[144] William J. Baumol. 2002. *The Free Market Innovation Machine*. Princeton, NJ: Princeton University Press, p. 20.

not only in customer contracts that are longer and fees that are higher than elsewhere in the world, but it has also allowed the carriers to control access, and to dictate what consumers can use. For example, this has dramatically impaired Research in Motion's (RIM) capacity to develop as well as it might have.[145]

Second, the Canadian market economy is small, open, dependent and balkanized. This entails that, given the technologically-defined minimum-optimum size of firms required for productive efficiency, greater industrial concentration ensues in small economies. This allows some market power in the hands of the few to have adverse effects on allocative efficiency through abuses of dominant position and high barriers to entry. This also dampens innovation, if firms do not fear outside entry. However, a 'little bit of bigness' may help productive efficiency through economies of scale and dynamic efficiency, by allowing firms to have some margin of maneuverability to mount successful R&D programs.[146]

On balance, the lack of competition in a small, open, dependent and balkanized socio-economy like Canada's has had a dampening effect on innovation, and consequently, such socio-economies have to find ways to minimize the undesirable and debilitating effects of concentrated market power, while supporting the dynamic, long-run market and non-market forces that help promote dynamic efficiency and innovation.[147]

---

[145] Michael Geist. 2011. "RIM's woes linked to policy," *Ottawa Citizen*, (August 23): D 1-2.

[146] Michal S. Gal. 2003. *Competition Policy for Small Market Economics*. Cambridge, MA: Harvard University Press, chapter 1; Harry C. Eastman and Stefan Stykolt. 1967. *The Tariff and Competition in Canada*. Toronto: Macmillan .

[147] Competitive forces do not suffice. Initiating and guiding creative conversations are also required for they are the wellsprings of creativity – that may not materialize without some public space being afforded (be it in the firm or in the industrial district) allowing these communities of practice to converse. This is possible only if something as loose as 'workable competition' permits (Richard K. Lester and Michael J. Piore. 2004. *Innovation – The Missing Dimension*. Cambridge, MA: Harvard University Press). In the case of Canada, an additional constraint has been imposed by the *Competition Act* that requires ensuring "that small- and medium-sized enterprises have an equitable opportunity to participate in the Canadian economy."

Why such failure?

The traditional policies have approached these problems in a dishevelled way.

A first approach has built on a variety of generic initiatives (like more generous tax credits for R&D, or more money devoted to higher education, etc.) that are not unreasonable or unhelpful *per se*, but they only develop potentialities. As such, they are not sufficient to catalyze the productivity and innovation nebulas that are subjected to a nexus of other forces and constraints, and there are too many blockages for any of these pointed initiatives to generate any momentum on their own.[148]

A second approach has amounted to vacuous calls for first ministers' conferences, for the creation of a national productivity and innovation council, or the equivalent of a Nobel Prize for innovators, or national roundtables, etc. that entail only useless evasive thinking and *babillage* at the top.[149]

There are many reasons for the failure of these approaches, but among the most important are (1) the fixation of policy-makers on the notion of a 'national' system of innovation and evasive macro-objectives (and the consequent occluding of the differential dynamics of the many local systems of innovations that make up the Canadian socio-economy in the design of public policy); and (2) the refusal to act in the face of the many forces that have contributed to dramatically reducing the invigorating pressures of robust competition in Canada.

(i) Canadian governments have had a fixation on the notion of a 'national' system of innovation, when, in fact, the texture of the productivity and innovation systems is a disintegrated bundle of networks of activities and institutions that have very little in the way

---

[148] Andrew Sharpe, 2007.

[149] Coalition for Action on Innovation in Canada. 2010. *An Action Plan for Prosperity*. Ottawa: CAIC; Public Policy Forum. 2011. *Innovation Next – Leading Canada to Greater Productivity, Competitiveness and Resilience*. Ottawa: Public Policy Forum.

of an organic wholeness.[150] This notional assemblage of an artificial whole leads to policies of *arrosage généralisé* over the whole system that have been costly, and often most ineffective, because the needs of local systems of innovation are quite diverse and require differentiated forms of support.

A more enlightened perspective would focus on development blocks, technology districts, sub-national forums, etc., where the learning is really occurring,[151] and would focus on the interactive mechanism between the search process and its environment: "both provide the source of differential fitness – firms whose R&D turns up more profitable processes of production or products will grow relative to their competitors – and also tend to bind them together as a community."[152]

The central notion of 'milieu' connotes three sets of forces: (1) the contours of a particular spatial set vested with a certain unity and tonus; (2) the organizational logic of a network of interdependent actors engaged in cooperative innovative activity; and (3) organizational learning, based on the dialectics between 'adapting actors' and the 'adopting milieu.'[153] These forces are deployed in response to competitive pressures.

It is not so much that public spending is inadequate. The problem has to do with the uptake and use of this support to generate private sector investments in R&D and commercialization that would produce increased productivity and more innovation.[154]

---

[150] Richard R. Nelson (ed). 1993. *National Systems of Innovation*. New York: Oxford University Press.

[151] This section draws freely from Gilles Paquet. 2005. *The New Geo-Governance – A Baroque Approach*. Ottawa: University of Ottawa Press, p. 121-124.

[152] Giovanni Dosi and Richard R. Nelson. 1994. "An Introduction to Evolutionary Theories in Economics," *Journal of Evolutionary Economics*, 4(3): 162.

[153] Denis Maillat. 1992. "Milieux et dynamique territorial de l'innovation," *Canadian Journal of Regional Science*, 15(2): 199-218.

[154] David Castle and Peter W.B. Phillips. 2011. "Science and Technology in Canada: Innovation Gaps and Productivity Traps," in Christopher Stoney and G. Bruce Doern, (eds.). *How Ottawa Spends 2011-12 – Trimming Fat or Slicing Pork?* Montreal: McGill-Queen's University Press, p. 163-179.

(ii) For a variety of reasons (size of the economy, miniature replica of the US structure in Canada, balkanization of the socio-economy, greater relative industrial concentration and market power of leading firms, fewer very large firms that could be the core of important networks, the softness of the *Competition Act*, the dominant view of the Republic of Science *à la* Michael Polanyi that is staunchly defended in most Canadian universities, etc.), the Canadian context has not been conducive to generating the sort of focus on competitive pressure that would generate a high productivity increase and innovation in the last few decades.[155]

There have been palavers of all sorts about promoting productivity and innovation, but these have been bizarrely focused on generalities like "being in the top 5 in the world" in one league or another, or economy-wide general measures, like rather blindly showering ever more money on higher education, without much attention being given to the real engines of productivity increase and innovation – which are competition and knowledge governance at the meso level. The philosophy of 'one-size-fits-all' has led to negligence in allowing key drivers of meso-innovation systems to fade away for fear (we presume) of creating precedents, or violating the canons of egalitarianism by intervening to sustain these sectoral champions.[156]

The way out

A more promising way is to approach the problems at the meso level with the tools of industrial organization: (1) potent inquiring systems designed to detect anomalies, and learn from failures, (2) failure correction as locally as one can, for the local

[155] Zhiqi Chen and Marc Duhamel (eds.). 2011. *Industrial Organization in Canada*. Montreal: McGill-Queen's University Press; Gilles Paquet. 2009. "Science Policy: Circumstantial Evidence," in *Crippling Epistemologies and Governance Failures – A Plea for Experimentalism*. Ottawa: University of Ottawa Press, p. 187-204.

[156] Department of Finance. 2006. *Advantage Canada: Building a Strong Economy for Canadians*. Ottawa: Department of Finance (www.fin.gc.ca); Industry Canada. 2007. *Mobilizing Science and Technology to Canada's Advantage*. Ottawa: Industry Canada, Science and Innovation Sector (ic.gc.ca/epublications).

systems vary greatly, and (3) appropriate 'safe-fail' mechanisms in all the learning loops.

The first priority is to tackle the knowledge governance challenge, that is, the daunting question of actively promoting governance structures and mechanisms (contracts, reward schemes, organizational culture, etc.) so as to favourably influence the processes of creating value-adding knowledge, and sharing, integrating and transferring it.[157] Whether these mechanisms are formal or informal, intra or inter-organizational, etc., the intelligence-innovation approach is geared to producing valuable new knowledge that will translate into productivity enhancement processes of various sorts. This entails a direction finding likely to finesse problem-finding and problem-solving, and the need to establish how explorative knowledge production should be governed.[158]

(i) It has been shown that it is not sufficient to change the rules of the game to make cooperation more attractive for selfish actors. Transforming the preferences may be necessary to overcome the social dilemmas of potential collaborators by "enabling intrinsic motivation." Setting incentives, targets and managerial control is likely to crowd out intrinsic motivation – intrinsic motivation is enhanced by communication opportunities, feedback mechanisms, procedural fairness, etc.[159]

(ii) Another lesson of the literature in knowledge governance is that one should question the overwhelming focus on infrastructure support, and

[157] Nicolai J. Foss and Snejina Michailova (eds.). 2009. *Knowledge Governance – Processes and Prospectives*. Oxford, UK: Oxford University Press.

[158] Margit Osterloh and Antoinette Weibel. 2009. "The Governance of Explorative Knowledge Production," in Nicolai J. Foss and Snejina Michailova (eds.). *Knowledge Governance – Processes and Prospectives*. Oxford, UK: Oxford University Press, p. 138-165.

[159] This would appear to raise serious questions about the government's approach over the last decades. Don Drummond ("Confessions of a Serial Productivity Researcher," *International Productivity Monitor*, 22, Fall 2011, p. 3-10) suggests that one must mobilize a coalition of researchers from all sectors to develop an inquiring system likely to help Canada out of this terrible Canadian productivity and innovation disaster.

education, training and university research (an area where Canada is already doing much more than its competitors), and to consider whether primary emphasis should not be on increasing the competitive pressure on the private sector, through eliminating a vast array of anti-competitive arrangements to ensure the existence of "workable competition" – while protecting in various ways the survival of the large firms that catalyze productive and innovative networks. They should not be allowed to be captured by foreign interests as a result of the vagaries of exchange rates, or a lack of due diligence by those charged with the protection of the public interest.

There have been efforts to sustain certain flagship firms in some sectors (Bombardier and Pratt & Whitney in the aeronautical industry, for instance), but there has not been a systematic and reliable information base that would enable a reasonable conversation on the merits of trading-off the 'external benefits' of such large firms (that constitute an important thrust, forcing productivity increase and innovation in the cluster of firms doing business with them) and the 'negative impacts' of the greater industrial concentration that they generate. As a result, Canada has proven particularly inept at times in this sort of balancing act: allowing too much laxness in the enforcement of strong competition, while being woefully indecisive (not to say criminally negligent) when it came to protecting a flagship firm (i.e., Connaught and Nortel).[160]

The second priority calls for local systems of innovation to become the new relevant units of analysis. Having different social foundations, the local systems respond to bottom-up dynamics through locally-based entities.[161] Many have tried

---

[160] The Connaught Laboratories had a significant hold on the North American vaccine market and Nortel was responsible for almost half of the business R&D expenditures: allowing the first one to be bought by a French state company and the other to be ruined by dismal management cannot be easily defended.

[161] Therefore vapid appeals to leadership (as if omniscient agents could be counted on to direct these processes top-down) are counter-productive (Kevin Lynch, 2011).

to promote such local perspectives (metropolitan technology councils, etc.) but they met with a deaf ear in Ottawa as a result of much dogmatic thinking by governments.[162]

Much has changed over the past twenty years, however. Communities of practice have become impressive operating units, and knowledge governance in the private sector has shown that meso-approaches are effective.[163] For instance, Caterpillar's Knowledge Network now has 3,000 tightly focused communities of practice involving more than half of its 70,000 worldwide employees. It has measured its success in impressive terms: 200 percent return on investment (ROI) for internal communities, and more than 700 percent ROI for its external communities.[164]

The third priority is to recognize that any experimentation is likely to fail, since there is no assurance that the right constellation of support and incentives will generate the requisite intrinsic motivation right from the start. It is

---

[162] Science Council of Canada. 1984. *Canadian Industrial Development: Some Policy Directions.* Ottawa: Supply & Services Canada; Charles H. Davis. 1991. *Local Initiatives to Promote Technological Innovation in Canada: Eight Case Studies.* Ottawa: The Science Council of Canada; Annalee Saxenian. 1994. *Regional Advantage.* Cambridge, MA: Harvard University Press; "L'économie des conventions," *Revue économique,* 40(2): 141-399; André Orléan. 1994. *Analyse économique des conventions.* Paris: Presses Universitaires de France; Bernard Enjolras. 2006. *Conventions et institutions.* Paris: L'Harmattan.

[163] Despite all this, it is surprising to note that recent efforts to shift attention "towards a no-frills, spend-where-it counts approach" to commercialization of research, to regional innovation clusters, and to small- and medium-sized firms in the 2010 federal budget, has generated scorn in a 'national' S&T establishment that is wedded to the defence of the 'national system.' The gospel in good currency supports the view that it is sufficient to feed the proverbial 'infrastructural horse' for it to take care of the local and regional 'sparrows,' and disparages targeted social learning initiatives as "the disregarded tactic of picking and replicating winners." David Castle and Peter W.B. Phillips, 2011.

[164] Vicki Powers. 2004. "Virtual Communities at Caterpillar Foster Knowledge Sharing," *Training & Development,* June (available at www.vickipowers.com/waitnps/virtualcommunities.htm).

therefore necessary to have in place *ab ovo* (i) strategies for learning as fast as possible from failures in the normal operations of the organizations at all levels (smaller learning loop in the face of change of degree), but also (ii) more radical 'safe-fail' provisions for abnormal times, when some essential variables would seem to be modified (larger learning loop in the face of change of kind).

On the first front, the approach to public policy based on intelligence and innovation would recognize that competitive pressure is likely to provide the true incentive to reveal anomalies and failures, to analyze them, and to experiment, so that pilot projects can show what will or will not work.[165] There is a need to ensure a level-playing field for Canadian enterprises, but this constitutes only a secondary supporting role.

On the second front, dramatic modifications of this kind may threaten the very future of the organization, and require decisive government intervention. The Connaught Laboratories and Nortel come to mind as instances of grievous failure to act in such circumstances.[166]

Has the attitude of the Canadian government been defendable in the face of these two Canadian giants being allowed to be sold to a European state company (in the first case) and being allowed to be destroyed by poor corporate strategy in a decade or so (in the second case)? We would argue that in neither case has the Canadian government acted wisely and in

---

[165] Amy C. Edmondson, 2011.

[166] (1) The Connaught Laboratories (a self-supporting, non-commercial part of the University of Toronto) was the first company to mass produce insulin in the 1920s and a large scale producer of the first Salk polio vaccine in the 1950s. In 1978, it acquired the research and production facilities of the Salk Institute. The Connaught Laboratories were a major player in the vaccine market in North America. It was sold by the University of Toronto to the Canadian Development Corporation in 1972. In 1989, the Connaught Laboratories were sold to Institut Mérieux (a state enterprise in France). (2) Nortel, a Canadian giant in telecom, collapsed as a result of disastrous strategies of adaptation to a turbulent world in the last 15 years. To gauge the importance of Nortel in Canada, it represented at times almost half of the whole expenditure on R&D of the Canadian private sector.

the public interest, and that 'safe-fail' mechanisms should have prevented these disasters.

The timidity of the Canadian government in the face of dramatic changes in the environment has allowed disastrous moves that could have been prevented. For instance, the government could have vetoed the sale of the Connaught Laboratories. And it should not have remained a by-stander as the most important private sector research engine in the country (Nortel) was being ruined by incompetent management. It should have used the same powers it would not have hesitated to use if any financial institution were to fall prey to the same incompetence: replacing the governing board in the name of public interest.

While this sort of 'death penalty' for misguided or mismanaged mega-companies might sound revolutionary, it would appear warranted when the most important engines of productivity and innovation of the country are under threat. To effect this dramatic change, the only thing that would be necessary is a modification of one line in the *Company Act* to allow such 'dechartering' under certain strict conditions. In fact, there is already a dechartering movement along those lines being argued by American legal scholars and judges.[167]

Conclusion

For decades, the traditional paradigm of public policy has been based on an overconfident philosophy of goal and control that has promised the moon. This approach has proved more and more ineffective in dealing with turbulent issue domains. In such a world, where problems are wicked and the ground is in motion, the conventional public policy process is most likely to fail.

The alternative view of the policy process as inquiring system (based on intelligence and innovation) would appear to

---

[167] Russell Mokhiber. 1998. "The Death Penalty for Corporations Comes of Age," *Business Ethics*, Nov-Dec (available at www.corpwatch.org/article. php?id=1810); Gilles Paquet. 2005. *Gouvernance: une invitation à la subversion.* Montreal: Liber, chapter 11.

be much better adapted to the modern context where power, resources and information are more widely distributed in many hands.[168] We have sketched a rough prototype of this new approach, insisting on the centrality of inquiring systems and 'safe-fail' mechanisms to ensure the best of social learning.

We have shown that this would result in shifting the public policy process in different directions in two areas where the failure of the traditional public policy process has been flagrant. Whether this alternative approach should be restricted to wicked policy problems (where probing search processes would appear to be the only way) or whether it should be more broadly used is a moot point. However, the question may become somewhat irrelevant if (as we suggest) all non-trivial public policy fields are in the process of becoming ever more wicked – that is, where the goals are ill-defined, and the means-ends relationships unstable, and therefore the traditional model most unhelpful.

---

[168] Gilles Paquet, 2009, *Scheming virtuously: the road to collaborative governance*, chapter 1.

| Metagovernance Review

Ruth Hubbard and Gilles Paquet

> "To be meaningful and relevant, this imperative,
> restorative and enhancing work of governance
> will need to draw from many minds, hearts and
> sources, and from many ranks including
> the law, political policy-makers, academics,
> multilateral institutions and managers."
> – *John Dalla Costa*

Introduction

The catastrophic public finance crisis in Ottawa in the early 1990s raised the spectre of Canada's having to transform its governance (effective coordination when power, resources and information are widely distributed) because it was showing signs of dysfunction. However, this quickly proved too daunting for federal politicians and bureaucrats. The exercise – labelled Program Review – instead morphed almost overnight into a public expenditures reduction *stricto sensu*, without much effort at governance modification.

Putting the federal fiscal house in order (in large part on the backs of the unsuspecting provinces, with ripple effects down to the municipalities) was much easier than dealing with the governance challenges. Provincial and municipal activities were disrupted, and little was done to make governance of the federal government or the country any more effective and innovative. In fact, not even all of the major cuts to federal government programs and operations *per se* could be regarded as intelligent or defendable. Rather, being seen to 'gore' everyone's 'ox' was defended as the only practical way to deal with the precarious fiscal situation. Thus, the old governing apparatus was left architecturally intact.

Consequently, as better economic times came, the refurbished margin of financial manoeuvrability generated by Program Review was merrily exploited by successive governments. Defective structures had not been systematically challenged, so when the next major fiscal crisis hit in the late 2000s, the governing apparatus could still be characterized as a black hole.[169]

Imposing the same shock treatment that was used in the 1990s is unlikely to work, given revived acrimonious federal-provincial relations, and the level of indebtedness of lower order governments. It would be politically immeasurably more costly to resolve fiscal problems by autocratically cutting transfers to provinces and savaging federal programs, while leaving the governing system untouched. The new setting calls for a new paradigm – the shift from big 'G' government to small 'g' governance: not simply doing the same with less, but finding ways to do things differently, if at all, and doing it collectively.[170]

In the rest of this chapter, we argue that this would call for a 'governance' review – a shift in the unit of analysis, a new approach, and a new strategy. We then illustrate in two case studies that opportunities exist for such an approach, and we indicate how it might work. Finally, we indicate under

[169] Ruth Hubbard and Gilles Paquet. 2010. *The Black Hole of Public Administration*. Ottawa: University of Ottawa Press.
[170] Ruth Hubbard and Gilles Paquet, 2010, p. 25.

which circumstances this approach is likely to be adopted, and what barriers would appear to exist to its being carried out successfully.

A new basic unit of analysis

The exercise of the mid 1990s scrutinized federal government programs to see: (1) if they were still required for the public interest; (2) whether other parties (coalitions of parties) could deliver them more effectively than the federal government; and (3) finally, if programs were felt to be required and most effectively delivered by the federal government, whether they could be despatched more efficiently and economically than heretofore, and whether they were still affordable for the Canadian federal government.[171]

The immense advantage of this approach (imposing a single standard across the board, ensuring that no program would escape scrutiny, and using units corresponding to the Treasury Board's financial accounting template) was matched by corresponding drawbacks, such as the focus on a relatively narrow unit of analysis, and avoidance of a serious scrutiny of the organizational dimension of the public sector. The priority was to make the exercise easily calculable; as a result, it allowed financial dimensions to trump all others. Unsurprisingly, the Treasury Board inherited what had been a Privy Council Office-initiated process.

Most unfortunate was the fact that, despite the convenience and expediency of this approach, it paid little attention to the collateral damage generated by program cuts on the issue domain within which the program was nested. In fact, the mid 1990s' experience inflicted much damage on many issue domains – damage that was momentous in many cases, even though it was not accurately measured by the 'bean counters.'

The Program Review approach was also crippled by its exclusive focus on instrumental rationality (i.e., on the narrow

---

[171] Gilles Paquet and Robert Shepherd. 1996. "The Program Review Process: A Deconstruction," in Gene Swimmer (ed.). *How Ottawa Spends 1996-97 – Life Under the Knife*. Ottawa: Carleton University Press, p. 39-72.

pursuit of calculable program objectives), ignoring the broader ecological rationality (i.e., the extent to which program cuts might or might not be in keeping with broader contextual concerns and needs, and might cause more damage than good, even financially). By partitioning issue domains into programs, governance concerns were unwittingly evacuated, and attention was focused on managerial plumbing, even where governance failures loomed large.

More importantly perhaps, the Program Review process was based on very static and stale notions of context and programs. They were analyzed as fixtures of a socio-economy at a point in time, with little or no concern for the dynamics of either the context, or the programs themselves, that is, for the evolving nature of the learning socio-economy, and the learning underpinning the programs in a context that is no longer Newtonian.

These drawbacks generated a perversion of the evaluation function that thus failed to fully take into account: (1) the new evolution of the learning socio-economy, innovation-mediated and innovation-driven, that transforms the context; (2) the new governance imperatives, based on social learning, that requires policies and programs to evolve as the context changes; and (3) the need to modify the substance and etiquette of evaluation in a context plagued with interactive complexity and 360-degree accountability, which requires an *ex ante* rather than an *ex post* focus.[172]

The shift to a learning socio-economy does not entail a change of degree, but rather a change of kind, and governing in such a context cannot be discussed in Newtonian terms (assuming well-defined goals, and a more or less placid environment, where the whole may be said to be the sum of the parts) in which the challenge could be regarded as designing control mechanisms likely to shift the organization toward certain desirable outcomes. Some problems are still tractable this way, but most are not.

---

[172] Gilles Paquet. 1999. "Auditing in a Learning Environment," *Optimum*, 29(1): 37-44.

In today's quantum world, a new way of thinking is required. There is no objective reality, the uncertainty principle looms large, events are at best probable, and the whole is a network of synergies and interactions among more or less self-organizing networks (i.e., the whole is quite different from the sum of the parts).[173] This has forced governance systems to become more modular, network-like, and to become integrated by informal moral contracts, building on a process of social learning through a critical multilogue among the stakeholders.[174]

In this new context, evaluation takes a new twist. It is not sufficient to operate *ex post*. What is needed is an *ex ante* appreciation of any action taken.[175] In this quantum world, the fixation on goals and control mechanisms is unhelpful. What is required is anticipatory appraisal work, quick feedback, and ongoing negotiated efforts to make the evolving expectations with partners explicit. If the value-added by appraisal is to be substantial, much of the work has to be reframed to focus on intelligence and innovation, not simply on goals and control. The focus of evaluation must be risk and exposure, and evaluation should not be regarded as a tool of compliance, but as a tool for change: improving the system's learning abilities and attenuating its learning disabilities. And since social learning proceeds faster when the process is decentralized, delayered and participative, and operating through a network of units that are sensitive to local circumstances, this sort of evaluation often leads to calls for organizational redesign.[176]

The new cosmology

The required new appreciative process must be designed to escape the limitations imposed by the focus on programs, on

[173] Thomas L. Becker. 1991. *Quantum Politics*. New York: Praeger.
[174] Gilles Paquet. 1999. *Governance Through Social Learning*. Ottawa: University of Ottawa Press.
[175] Charles F. Sabel. 2001. "A Quiet Revolution of Democratic Governance: Towards Democratic Experimentalism," in Wolfgang Michalski et al. (eds), *Governance in the 21st Century*. Paris: OECD, p. 121-148.
[176] Gilles Paquet, 1999, *Governance Through Social Learning*.

instrumental rationality, and on strict financial imperatives alone, and to focus instead on issue domains as the unit of analysis, on ecological rationality, and organization learning and redesign – in the search for guideposts for required actions.[177]

This does not mean that short-run financial considerations of all sorts must be irresponsibly sideswiped. Rather, sudden savage financial cuts become only a subset of levers among many, and resolving financial problems is no longer framed as an issue tractable only by mechanical short-term cuts, but defined more wisely and in a longer run perspective as maybe tractable by governance repairs. Indeed, this is often the only reasonable way to proceed.

The new cosmology entails a new way of defining the problems:

1. by dealing directly with 'issue domains' (not programs) to provide a broader platform (in time and space) for reframing, restructuring and retooling the portfolios;
2. by focusing first on issue domains where the federal government and the provinces are substantially involved in *de facto* composite jurisdictions, for these areas are those most likely to suffer from coordination failures;
3. by reducing waste through doing the governing work more effectively (recognizing the diversity of circumstances and premises).

Our main objective in this chapter is to illustrate how such an approach might work. This will be done in three phases. First, we briefly raise a few general questions about the new dimensions of interest that need to be taken into account, as well as about the general coherence of the approach. Second, we examine two cases to show how one might be able to conduct such an analysis and what general results one might expect, even on the basis of a very provisional query. Third, we draw some lessons learned

---

[177] Ruth Hubbard and Gilles Paquet, 2010, p. 461; Gerd Gigerenzer. 2001. "The Adaptive Toolbox," in G. Gigerenzer and R. Selten (eds). *Bounded Rationality – The Adaptive Toolbox*. Cambridge, MA: The MIT Press, p. 37-50.

from these case studies about the promises and difficulties of a true metagovernance review.

A framework

Outline of the inquiry and nature of the issue domains
This is not meant to be a template mechanically used in approaching issue domains, with a view to proceeding with a governance review. As will become obvious in the two examples we analyze in the next section (mental health, and the problems created by the Mohawk cross-border interface zone), there is much that must remain idiosyncratic in any governance approach to issue domains. Yet some basic questions would appear to be fundamentally important in most cases when using this approach (as set out in Figure 8).

FIGURE 8.
Basic Questions for a Fundamental Governance Review Approach

STAGE	TASKS
I	• Identification of the relevant issue domains • Empirical evidence of dysfunction at the issue domain level & identification of the sources of the dysfunction
II	• Strategic focus of intervention • Major sources of leverage • Stages of intervention
III	• Short-term impact, long-term impact and feedback expected • Risk exposure and 'fail-safe' mechanisms

First, relevant issue domains are socio-technical systems that are most often the locus of overlapping jurisdictions. The interactions within the issue domain can be expected to be more densely integrated within the domain than the interactions with other segments of the social system. Moreover, to be fruitful, the inquiry must be guided by observable empirical evidence of dysfunction, along with some sense of its sources, and the extent to which different actors can be identified as potentially responsible for part of the dysfunction.

Second, it must be possible to identify a useful focus (or a small number of foci) of intervention for promoting more effective coordination and social learning, and the sort of tools that are likely to be of use.

Third, one must be able to map out the required stages of intervention, the likely impact of such action in the short and long run, the nature of the risk exposure, and the 'fail-safe' and 'safe-fail' mechanisms likely to be necessary if disastrous derailing is to be avoided.

The Clark et al. study of higher education in Ontario would qualify as an interesting and well-carried out study of an issue domain.[178] It deals with (1) overlapping jurisdictions, and a loosely integrated socio-technical system that gives clear signs of dysfunction, and the sources of dysfunction are unearthed; (2) foci for intervention, levers and stages of intervention are identified; and (3) expected short-term and long-term impacts are gauged. The only elements that would appear to be absent from this otherwise impressive study are an evaluation of risk exposure if the proposed changes were initiated and some suggestions of 'fail-safe' and 'safe-fail' mechanisms to mitigate the risks of failure.

Self-organizing networks as a way to map issue domains

To help fix ideas, an issue domain could be defined operationally as a *de facto* self-organizing network. To use the language of Walter J.M. Kickert et al., in most significant situations "public policy is made and implemented in networks of interdependent actors ... [i]n a network situation a single central authority, a hierarchical ordering and a single organizational goal do not exist." The consequence is that improving governance of these networks means "improving the conditions under which actors interact."[179]

[178] Ian D. Clark et al. 2009. *Academic Transformation – The Forces Reshaping Higher Education in Ontario.* Montreal/Kingston: McGill-Queen's University Press; Gilles Paquet. 2010. "Ontario Higher Education as Governance Failures," *www.optimumonline.ca*, 40(1): 60-66.
[179] Walter J.M. Kickert et al. (eds.). 1997. *Managing Complex Networks: Strategies for the Public Sector.* London, UK: Sage Publications, p. 2, 10-11.

In situations in which government decides to try to nudge the networks that provide the structure and performance of an issue domain in certain directions, steering efforts may take many forms. Two of the main ones are 'negotiating' (with the government trying to act as a mediating agent of change), or 'building new relations' (with the government taking on the job of bridge-building and enriching the communication infrastructure in order to facilitate or enable more effective mediation and/or negotiation in the future).[180]

There are obviously many other ways for government to 'instantiate its nudging function.'[181] We limit ourselves to these two avenues in making this preliminary case for the workability of a true governance review because they appear to be available and promising.

Two cases

The two cases sketched below are not fully developed blueprints of how to conduct a governance review, but simply an attempt to establish that the approach is both plausible and promising in the case of two particularly thorny problem areas.

The mental health portfolio and the Mohawk cross-border interface zone are used as illustrations because they create challenges that have not been adequately dealt with to-date, and they promise immense financial benefits from governance re-arrangements in the medium-term. Moreover, they offer a good illustration of each of the two main routes identified in the last section.

The mental health initiative

The World Health Organization (WHO) has defined mental health as: "a state of well-being in which the individual realizes his or her own abilities, can cope with the normal stresses of

---

[180] Walter J.M. Kickert and Joop F.M. Koppenjan. 1997. "Public Management and Network Management: An Overview," in *Managing Complex Networks: Strategies for the Public Sector*. Walter J.M. Kickert et al. (eds). London, UK: Sage Publications, p. 35-61.

[181] Richard H. Thaler and Cass R. Sunstein. 2008. *Nudge*. New Haven: Yale University Press.

life, can work productively and fruitfully, and is able to make a contribution to his or her community."[182]

In their 2001 report, "The Global Burden of Disease Study," the WHO, the World Bank, and Harvard University estimated that 10.5 percent of the total burden of disease worldwide can be accounted for by mental illness, potentially increasing to almost 15 percent in 2020. The WHO also noted "the economic burden of mental illness is wide-ranging, long-lasting and huge – but remains largely underestimated."[183]

Issue domain, dysfunction, and sources of dysfunction
Epidemiological information suggests that 3 percent of the population in Canada will experience a serious mental illness, and another 17 percent will experience mild to moderate mental illness.[184] Virtually all Canadians will be touched by it, directly or indirectly. It is certainly an issue domain of national interest.

In 1998, the economic burden of mental illnesses in Canada was conservatively estimated at $6.3 billion in direct costs (i.e., health care) and $8.1 billion in indirect costs (lost productivity, of which $6 billion is related to short-term disability).[185] In 1998, mental illness accounted for 4.9 percent of the overall

---

[182] World Health Organization. 2001. "Mental Health: strengthening mental health promotion." Fact Sheet No. 229, (November). http://www.who.int/mediacentre/factsheets/fs220/en/, quoted in the *Final Report of the Standing Senate Committee on Social Affairs, Science and Technology*, "Out of the Shadows at Last: Transforming Mental Health, Mental Illness and Addiction Services in Canada," Kirby Report, 2006. Ottawa: Senate of Canada, p. 412.

[183] World Health Organization, the World Bank and Harvard University. 2001. "The Global Burden of Disease Study" (November) and the World Health Organization. 2001. "Mental Health: New Understanding, New Hope", are both quoted in the *Interim Report of the Senate Standing Committee on Social Affairs, Science And Technology*. "Mental Health, Mental Illness and Addiction: Overview of Policies and Programs in Canada," Kirby Report, 2004. Ottawa: Senate of Canada, p. 102.

[184] "Out of the Shadows at Last," Kirby Report, 2006, p. 50.

[185] "Mental Health, …, Kirby Report, 2004, p. 101.

direct and indirect cost of disease in Canada, while in terms of direct costs alone, mental illness ranked second only to cardiovascular disease.[186]

Nearly 50 years ago, the Canadian Mental Health Association stated: "(i)n no other field, except perhaps leprosy, has there been as much confusion, misdirection and discrimination against the patient, as in mental illness."[187] The Senate Standing Committee on Social Affairs, Science and Technology (the Kirby Committee) reported hearing thousands of personal stories demonstrating the applicability of those remarks to the current situation. Moreover, the Kirby Committee reported in 2006 that "despite recent actions by several provincial governments [that] have begun to focus a long-overdue spotlight on mental health, it remains that the whole complex, pervasive problem of mental illness and addiction in Canadian society continues to be neglected."[188]

It also noted that no single level of government has the sort of resources of all sorts necessary for dealing with the full range of mental health issues on its own; that mental health problems and substance abuse disorders are responsible for a large proportion of all diminished workplace productivity, absenteeism and disability in workplaces of all sectors (costing Canadian companies in the order of $18 billion a year recently); and that the proportion of workplace disability due to mental illness and substance abuse is increasing more rapidly than those relating to other illnesses.[189]

In its first report in late 2004, the Kirby Committee recognized "that the mental health and addiction system is not, in fact, a real system but rather a complex array of services delivered through federal, provincial and municipal jurisdictions and private providers, including initiatives by

[186] "Mental Health, ...", Kirby Report, 2004, p. 101.
[187] Quoted in "Out of the Shadows at Last," Kirby Report, 2006, p. xvii.
[188] "Out of the Shadows at Last," Kirby Report, 2006, p. 435.
[189] "Out of the Shadows at Last," Kirby Report, 2006, p. 435-436.

individuals with mental illness/addictions themselves. This system is a mix of acute care services in general hospitals, specialized services for specific disorders or populations, outpatient community clinics, community-based services providing psychosocial supports (housing, employment, education and crisis intervention) and private counseling, all of varying capacity, often operating in silos, and all-too-frequently disconnected from the health care system."[190]

The result is that, "in most jurisdictions, a highly fragmented (non) system has become increasingly difficult to navigate by both individuals with mental illness and addiction, and service providers. Compounding this fragmentation is ... [the fact] that ... data information systems are not yet adequately linked across the sectors concerned (e.g., health, housing, education, family benefits, work environment etc.)."[191]

Five issues were identified by the Kirby Committee as contributing importantly to the dysfunction of the mental health non-system: (1) 'governance' (poor coordination); (2) chaotic service delivery systems; (3) insufficient research; (4) no straightforward way, across the country, to exchange best practices and research syntheses about the organization and the delivery of mental health prevention, treatment, rehabilitation and support service for knowledge producers and users; and (5) stigma and discrimination.

The federal government has an important and direct role to play (e.g., for status Indians, veterans and federal public servants). Notwithstanding the jurisdictional disputes, it also has a long-standing interest in healthcare, (including financial) as part of its responsibility for the long-term well-being of Canadians, by promoting productivity and economic growth.

---

[190] "Mental Health," Kirby Report, 2004, p. 153.
[191] "Mental Health," Kirby Report, 2004, p. 153.

Strategy in many stages

The Kirby Committee revealed the existence of a *de facto* not-very well functioning self-organizing network: a forum where all interested parties could contribute to problem definition. By conducting its business in an open-ended way, the Kirby Committee succeeded in allowing the necessary common ground for public action to emerge, while taking fully into account the inherent complexity, variety and flexibility required in a broad and sweeping strategy.

The committee put forward 117 recommendations in all, directed at all levels of government, as well as at providers of mental health services and support. It made recommendations on issues falling outside the federal jurisdiction, arguing that "no effective, systematic approach to the delivery of mental health and addiction services could have been made otherwise."[192]

Despite all the issues identified as sources of the mental health system dysfunction, improving governance was the central concern. The Kirby Committee also adopted a long-term view, one that did not fall prey to the propensity to centralize in the name of supposedly necessary 'national' (the code word for 'federal') strategies. What was felt necessary was better coordination and, at a minimum, a facilitating or enabling function (at least in a transition period) to ensure a needed focus on mental health issues.

The committee argued forcefully for the creation of the Canadian Mental Health Commission (CMHC), a recommendation supported by almost all the stakeholders and all provincial and territorial governments, except Quebec. Even the opposition health critic in Ottawa gave support, and there was "universal enthusiasm [for its creation from] ...those concerned with mental health in Canada."[193]

---

[192] "Out of the Shadows at Last," Kirby Report, 2006, p. 431.
[193] "Out of the Shadows at Last," Kirby Report, 2006, p. 432.

The subsequent creation of the commission and its funding for a 10-year transition period entailed:

i)   an independent not-for-profit organization, at arm's length from governments and all existing mental health stakeholders, (with a central focus on those living with mental illness and their families; building on complementing initiatives already underway; establishing cross-sectoral partnerships; emphasizing evidence-based policies and service delivery methods; calling for rigorous evaluation, assessment of its own activities, and regular reporting);

ii) a clear statement of its mission (e.g., facilitator, enabler and supporter; catalyst for reform of policies and improvements in service delivery; source of information for all, and educator of Canadians);

iii) a board that was arm's length from governments and interest groups, and well-balanced advisory committees.[194]

In November 2009, the commission released a framework strategy document entitled *Toward Recovery and Well-Being*, drawing on the experience and ideas of thousands of people.[195] Since then, it has begun work at public engagements through round tables, online consultations on key topics, and other engagement initiatives, with a view to translating the framework into a strategic plan aimed at completion by the end of 2012.

Impacts, risks and 'fail-safe' mechanisms
The central question is: what can be done to deal as effectively as possible with the 'cost containment' of government spending, and the 'cost effectiveness' of the efforts deployed?

[194] "Out of the Shadows at Last," Kirby Report, 2006, p. 437-442.
[195] Mental Health Commission of Canada. 2009. *Toward Recovery and Well-being: A Framework for a Mental Health Strategy for Canada* available at http://www.mentalhealthcommission.ca/SiteCollectionDocuments/boarddocs/15507_MHCC_EN_final.pdf [accessed October 5, 2010].

The Kirby Committee tackled the question of how to deal relatively effectively and efficiently with the transition period to a more cost-effective public investment in mental health by dealing, *inter alia*, with two of the costliest items: (1) shifting those individuals currently treated as in-patients in hospitals into community-based care where they would do better; and (2) bringing the percentage of those without affordable housing down to match general levels (something the committee became convinced was essential).[196]

Their estimate of the transition cost was $2.4 billion over 10 years, but savings as a result of the transition can be estimated from $.5 billion up to $2 billion *annually*, beginning with the transition period, making the benefit/cost ratio acceptable.[197]

The transition strategy is not without risks. The first is that the actual transition costs may rise uncontrollably, with governments being pressed to increase expenditures. The second is that the megacommunity might not (or will not) shake off its sense of 'entitlement', and might also apply immense pressure for an even greater government investment in this issue domain. These pressures are likely to be strong in

[196] The Kirby Committee pointed out that "(s)omewhere between 30% and 40% of homeless people have mental health problems" (2006: 118) and heard from witnesses that "housing is protection from illness ... from the vagaries of mental illness, from the voices, from the fears ... [and that] supported housing ...is ... cost-effective ... [and] works" (2006: 119-120). "Out of the Shadows at Last," Kirby Report, 2006, p. 118-123.

[197] The Institute of Health Economics and the Alberta Health Services Report. September 2008. "How Much Should Be Spent on Mental Health?" provides a rough estimate (which they say is consistent with the Kirby Report) and assumes that service cost in the hospital (old) and community (new) modes of care are the same. Overall savings would be $.5 billion annually after a 5 year transition. The source of the funds for the new (community) care, however, would not necessarily be part of publicly funded health care costs. As a result, the savings could be estimated to be up to 20% (the size of the shift of the treated population) of the base cost of the Kirby Report's $10 bilion in the last year of the transition (including population growth). §5.5, p. 44-47. http://www.ihe.ca/documents/Spending%20on%20Mental%20Health%20Final.pdf [accessed October 5, 2010].

a context where health care *in toto* is possibly already taking quite a large share of public spending.

In its recent economic survey of Canada, the OECD warned that "[i]n the longer run the soundness of Canada's finances will likely be largely determined by the decisions taken regarding the health care system ... [which] offers high-quality services to all residents ... at relatively high cost. ... With health care already accounting for around half of total provincial primary spending, meeting the fiscal and demographic challenges will require that the growth of public spending be reduced from an annual rate of about 8% seen over the last decade, toward the trend rate of growth of nominal income in coming years (estimated to be less than 4% per year), the only alternative being to squeeze other public spending or to raise taxes or user charges" (italics removed).[198]

This should act as a serious forewarning, and encourage the country to tackle the governance of healthcare as a priority, and as well, given the existing culture of entitlements, to put in place strict measures of cost containment, both for the transition period and in the steady state that will follow. There needs to be a publicly-announced strict ceiling (i) on the state share of health costs (and perhaps on the federal portion of that share); (ii) on the total costs of the transition phase in the refurbishment of the mental health regime; and (iii) on mental health costs as a proportion of healthcare costs in steady state (e.g., the 6.1 percent share of total government spending on healthcare of $91.4 billion that was estimated by the Institute for Health Economics to have been in place in 2003-04).[199]

With respect to pressure for greater government investment in mental health after the transition period, the up to $2 billion

---

[198] In fact, a recent OECD report points out that there is ample scope for efficiency savings and quality improvements. OECD. 2010. "OECD Economic Surveys: Canada, overview." Economic and Development Review Committee of the OECD, p. 9-10. http://www.oecd.org/dataoecd/23/38/45950025.pdf.

[199] The Institute of Health Economics and the Alberta Health Services Report, 2008, p. 25. It notes that public spending on mental health in 2003-2004 was 6.1% while the European benchmark for a minimum optimal allocation is 5%.

of anticipated annual savings (accruing to provinces/territories) ought to be clearly identified in the appropriate fiscal frameworks to show citizens that, indeed, savings have been possible, rather than simply allowing them to disappear unaccounted for, in an ever expanding health care expenditure vortex.

The Mohawk Cross-Border Interface Zone

What we call the Mohawk cross-border interface zone connotes a complex nexus of places and peoples: geography (governments at three levels in two countries), First Nations (FN) – especially the Mohawk Nation (MN), the Haudenosaunee (the Six Nations Iroquois Confederacy (SNC), of which the Mohawk Nation is a member), and the groups involved with them directly or not.

The Mohawk Nation itself connotes several communities in the four geographic areas of Ontario, Quebec and upstate New York.[200] Of these, the main areas of interest for the purposes of this case centre on the Six Nations of the Grand River (which is home to members of all six Iroquois nations, and is comprised of two reserves) to the west, the Kahnawake to the east, as well as the Bay of Quinte (Tyendinaga) east of Belleville, and the Akwesasne/St Regis in the middle, spanning the Canada-United States (as well as Ontario-Quebec) borders. In particular, the 14-mile stretch of the St. Lawrence River poses particularly difficult challenges in terms of government enforcement of border security and oversight of the tobacco trade. Indeed, the tobacco issue may serve as a most useful exemplar of the problems posed in and by this zone.

Issue domain, dysfunction and sources of dysfunction

As the main cause of preventable illness, disability and death in Canada, tobacco and tobacco products are highly controlled by governments (e.g., federal control of the manufacture, sale, labeling and promotion, and varying provincial regulation of sale and promotion of the industry). It is currently estimated

---

[200] Included are six Canadian FN reserves under the *Indian Act* (Kanesatake, Kahnawake, Akwesasne, Six Nations of Grand River (two reserves), Tyendinaga and Wahta Mohawk) and three in the U.S. (Ganienkeh, Kanatsiohareke, and St. Regis, which borders Akwesasne).

that nearly 18 percent of people 15 years and older in Canada smoke (a rate at least two or three times higher for Aboriginal people). The tobacco industry is also an important source of federal/provincial tax revenue (almost $7 billion (split 40:60 between orders of government) in 2007-2008.[201] The industry in Canada still involves 100+ licensed growers and tens of thousands of small convenience stores, gas stations, etc., who sell these products, some of which get as much as 40 percent of their sales from tobacco sales.

Unfortunately however, despite having what the World Health Organization asserts as one of the best regulatory regimes for tobacco control,[202] recent data show that, while smoking has declined slightly in Canada between 2002 and 2008, the estimated percentage of contraband sales appears to have grown from 10 to 31 percent during the same time period.[203]

As of July 1, 2010, the price of a carton of cigarettes (including taxes) was between $70 and $106 (depending on the provincial/territorial tax rate), while the same quantity of illegal cigarettes could be bought for as little as $6.[204]

In 2008, it was estimated that the cost in lost government revenues was $1.6 billion.[205] Moreover, contraband has been linked to drug trafficking and terrorism, involving (directly or indirectly) groups such as the Hells Angels, the Russian mafia,

---

[201] $6.969 billion, excluding sales taxes according to public accounts or budgets as reported by Physicians for a Smoke-Free Canada in December 2008 http://www.smoke-free.ca/factsheets/pdf/totaltax.pdf [accessed 17/9/2010].

[202] World Health Organization. 2005. "Regulation of Tobacco Products: Canada Report", WHO Study Group on Tobacco Regulation, Geneva Switzerland. http://www.escholarship.org/uc/item/4zd2n223?display=all.

[203] Smoke Free Canada. 2010. "Estimating the volume of contraband sales of tobacco in Canada – updated April 2010," research paper of Physicians for a Smoke-Free Canada, Ottawa, Canada http://www.smoke-free.ca/pdf_1/2010/Estimating%20the%20volume%20of%20Contraband%20Sales%20of%20Tobacco%20in%20Canada-2009.pdf [accessed 17/9/2010].

[204] National Post Editorial Board. 2010. "An economic cancer," *National Post*, September 17.

[205] John Ivison. 2008. "Ottawa needs U.S. help to fight illegal tobacco," *National Post*, May.

and Hezbollah.[206] Despite the seemingly dramatic increase in contraband and its costs for the state, a Health Canada survey has pointed out that: "part of the public doesn't believe it is illegal to buy these cigarettes."[207]

The Cornwall, Ontario area has been called "ground zero" of the contraband trade. The RCMP has reported that the St. Lawrence River in the Cornwall-Akwesasne/St Regis area "has traditionally been used to smuggle contraband to and from Canada due to its geographic and political complexity ... from Canada into the U.S. [mainly] marijuana, ecstasy and illegal migrants while weapons, cocaine and contraband cigarettes are moved from the U.S. into Canada. This area continues to be exploited by organized crime groups from large centres such as Montreal, Ottawa, and Toronto."[208] Not unreasonably, however, cracking down on tobacco smuggling is a lower priority for the FN policing at Akwesasne and St Regis than drugs, money laundering and human trafficking.

The Fraser Institute recently noted that, fed by unlawful manufacture of cigarettes in the United States on Aboriginal territories that border Canada (primarily at Askwesasne), tobacco products designated for sale on FN reserves that are diverted to the black market are among the primary sources of contraband tobacco.[209]

The FN argue that much of this activity is not really illegal, because "(s)ome tobacco routes [e.g., within the Mohawk Nation territory] have existed for centuries ... [so that] selling tax-

---

[206] National Post Editorial Board, 2010.

[207] François Damphousse, Director, Quebec Office of the Non-smokers' Rights Association, May 14, 2008 testimony to the Standing Committee on Public Safety and National Security.

[208] RCMP. 2007. "Federal Tobacco Control Strategy (FTCS): The Illicit Tobacco Market in Canada January – December 2006." http://www.rcmp-grc.gc.ca/pubs/tobac-tabac/ftcs-sflt-eng.pdf [accessed 18/9/2010].

[209] Natchum Gabler and Diane Katz. 2010. "Contraband Tobacco in Canada: Tax Policies and Black Market Incentives," Studies in Risk and Regulation. Vancouver, BC: Fraser Institute, http://www.fraserinstitute.org/uploadedFiles/fraser-ca/Content/research-news/research/publications/contraband-tobacco-in-canada(1).pdf.

exempt cigarettes [on reserves to all customers, First Nations and not] is not perceived as a criminal activity, but rather as a form of economic development ...[and in fact] their [FN] community is being unfairly criminalized by law enforcement and government."[210]

Importantly, the Aboriginal tobacco industry of late 2010 appears to have become a force unto itself. There are said to be nearly 200 'smoke shacks' in the communities of the Mohawk Nation, plus several clandestine factories. This underscores reports that "[a] growing number of plants ... are firmly ensconced on some Canadian reserves where risky, international smuggling is not necessary to get the finished goods to market. That includes the Canadian side of Akwesasne and Tyendinaga ... the RCMP say."[211]

Criminal activity is not confined to reserves; it is reported that contraband cigarettes can be bought under the counter from urban retailers and (through dealers) in coffee shops and schoolyards in Canadian cities.[212] Nevertheless, the geographic and political complexities related to the tobacco industry in the Mohawk zone create a major challenge.

Strategy in many stages

In the Mohawk zone case (as opposed to the mental health case), what is involved is not simply initiating negotiations (with government behaving as a party like the others, and acting as an agent of change), but rather with government having to take on the job of enriching the communication infrastructure, in order to make possible effective mediation and negotiation.

The central issue is access by the Mohawk Nation to revenue generation in a particularly complex and challenging

[210] J. Sweeting et al. 2009. "Anti-Contraband Policy Measures: Evidence for Better Practice – Summary Report," Special Report Series. Toronto, ON: The Ontario Tobacco Research Unit, June, p. 35-36. http://www.otru.org/pdf/special/special_anti_contraband_measures_summary.pdf [accessed 19/9/2010].

[211] Tom Blackwell. 2010. "Native-made cigarettes bring wealth and disapproval to reserves," *National Post*, September 17.

[212] National Post Editorial Board, 2010.

context. On the one hand, FN have a stake in reducing on-reserve criminal activity and in controlling the use of tobacco products by their members, while on the other hand, they see the dominium in this issue domain as intimately connected to their sovereignty and their right to govern themselves, as well as being one of the very few sources of economic activity and revenue generation in parts of their territory.

As Jerry Montour, Chief Executive of Grand River Enterprises, testified to the Standing Committee on Public Safety and National Security,[213] "the only opportunities that present good employment on our First Nation territories right now are tobacco-related."

It is clear that, in some Mohawk communities, legal activities generate significant annual revenue (e.g., Six Nations of the Grand River, through the fourth-largest licensed cigarette manufacturer in Canada. Grand River Enterprise, has ploughed an estimated $1 million back into economic development for the reserve, and sent $500 million to the government) and Kahnawake's Morris Mohawk Gaming Group brings in a large (unknown) amount of annual revenue, and may or may not plough a portion back into the community. Nevertheless, young people are said to be able to "earn $2,000 a week acting as a runner [for illicit tobacco]... [while being] untouchable, because they are under eighteen".[214]

This suggests that any possibility of effective mediation and negotiation with these First Nations needs to be rooted in first establishing 'a basis for partnership' with Mohawk governments, something that, in testimony to the Standing Committee on Public Safety and National Security, Mr. Mike Mitchell, former Grand Chief of the Mohawk Council of Akwesasne, described as "something [that] is going to be enacted that will, in a safe way, guarantee the safety of your

---

[213] Testimony to the Standing Committee on Public Safety and National Security, May 12, 2008.

[214] Michel Gadbois, senior vice-president, Canadian Convenience Store Association, testifying to the Standing Committee on Public Safety and National Security, May 14, 2008.

people and ours ... (and) our ability to create our own laws and allow us to apply them."[215]

What seems to be required is a two-stage strategy following the lead of the successful approach used between the government of Quebec and the Mohawk at Kahnawake in mid 2009 to deal, *inter alia*, with "tobacco, petroleum and alcohol products", as well as "fiscal matters related to consumer goods and services" (presumably including Internet gaming).[216]

The genesis of such a document would pose a daunting task. Governments involved would necessarily include the government of New York State (and possibly the federal government of the U.S.), as well as that of Canada, Ontario and Quebec, while the Mohawk Nation's interests would require, at a minimum, representatives from the Mohawk Nation Council of Chiefs (MNCC) or the Haudenosaunee Grand Council of Chiefs (HGCC), part of their historic (ongoing) governance regime.

The first stage might include the establishment of a small 'wise persons' group which would act as enabler, facilitator, and supporter of the development of a covenant of the most general sort (as exemplified by the Quebec document, provided as an appendix to this chapter). The aim would be to create, cooperatively, a statement of mutual respect and understanding, including symbolic measures and an expression of willingness to develop financial and fiscal arrangements providing for long-term economic stability, as well as a framework agreement to establish the protocol to arrive at sectoral arrangements that include fiscal matters related to tobacco and tobacco products.

The second stage would involve the negotiation *per se*. A number of principles would likely shape the intentions of the

---

[215] Testimony to the Standing Committee on Public Safety and National Security, June 4, 2008.

[216] "Statement of understanding and mutual respect" signed June 10, 2009, and "Framework Agreement between Québec and the Mohawks of Kahnawake" signed July 16, 2009.

http://www.autochtones.gouv.qc.ca/relations_autochtones/ententes/mohawks/ententes_mohawks_en.htm accessed 18/9/2010.

Canadian and U.S. governments in subsequent negotiations: (i) providing practical sovereignty with respect to tobacco control (by transferring significant authority and decision-making to the MNCC/HGCC with respect to tobacco control on MN territory); (ii) investing significant government resources in efforts aimed at enabling, inciting and supporting good governance for the MN in the area of tobacco control; (iii) foreseeing significant revenue sharing of proceeds from improved tobacco control accruing to Mohawk nations and others living in Mohawk territory, and governments; and (iv) not penalizing the MN unduly (financially) for the revenue earned with any new arrangement, in basic areas currently funded by Canadian governments, such as health and education.

The financial costs of this approach have been estimated at federal expenditure of about $19 million over three years for the operation of the new governance mechanism, and an expenditure of $1 million in year four for the evaluation of results. The outcome is estimated to be a reduction of fiscal leakage by 40 percent (a combination of higher prices and better control), yielding an estimated minimum of $1 billion annually. Of this, $500 million would be sent to governments, and the remainder would be kept by the HGCC/MNCC to be distributed as it sees fit, with agreed upon appropriate accountability.[217] The government expenditures could be recovered by the end of year two.

Impacts, risks and 'fail-safe' mechanisms

This issue domain remains troublesome for reasons of its own: "[t]he easy availability of cheap contraband tobacco ... undermines the two primary objectives of federal and provincial excise taxes on tobacco: reducing smoking prevalence and generating government revenue."[218] The question again is how

---

[217] The independent public policy think tank, The Frontier Centre for Public Policy, publishes a voluntary "Aboriginal Governance Index" annually that provides a very good example of what is possible, and might stimulate useful ideas.

[218] Natchum Gabler and Diane Katz, 2010.

to deal as effectively as possible with the 'cost containment' (in this case, of government losses, and pleas for government funding flowing from its inability to enforce its own laws), as well as the 'cost-effectiveness' of continuing to rely primarily on the coercive power of government when "the underlying problem ... [is to] somehow reconcile Aboriginal territorial autonomy and treaty rights with Canadian law."[219]

At the same time, there seems to be willingness on the part of key elements of the Mohawk Nation leadership to accept Canadian sovereignty and, by extension, there is a need to begin to tackle difficulties on MN territory caused by external lawless drivers (i.e., the heads of organized crime).

There are, however, those who do not agree, and herein lies the main risk. The Mohawk Warrior Society poses the highest risks. Its members are responsible for defence and security in the territory of Kahnawake, but their Facebook site now states that they "defend the rights and interests of all native peoples of Canada, in solidarity with liberation and decolonization movements around the world."[220] Its members emerged in the early 1970s as highly idealistic, aiming at safeguarding traditional values and upholding native land claims to sovereignty.

By 1996, however, the Mackenzie Institute noted that they had "come a long way from the inspired militants of 1973 ... the true legacy of the Mohawk Warriors Society [is the Manitoba Warriors and the Indian Posse of Manitoba]: armed teenage drug dealers who believe that they need respect neither Canadian laws, the traditional authorities of the First Nations, nor the peaceful intentions of their own people."[221] It would not be surprising if this had become the view of at least some members of the Warrior Society itself.

---

[219] Natchum Gabler and Diane Katz, 2010, p. 37.
[220] See for example, http://www.facebook.com/pages/Mohawk-Warrior-Society/35272274775#!/pages/Mohawk-Warrior-Society/35272274775?v=info [accessed September 20, 2010].
[221] "The Long Fall of the Mohawk Warriors," http://www.mackenzieinstitute.com/1996/1996_06_Military_Mohawks.html [accessed September 20, 2010].

The 'fail-safe' mechanism lies in the conditions of control that the Mohawk Nation uses to circumscribe activities related to its own police. There is some hope that this approach might offer sufficient reassurance about a diminished threat to the national defence of the Mohawk Nation that such control would be reasonably effective, both in terms of cross-border traffic in contraband tobacco, as well as in reducing the prevalence of smoking tobacco products emanating from it.

Lessons learned

Our intent is not to derive a protocol for conducting a metagovernance review from these two cases. Rather, it is to draw attention to some of the promises and difficulties of a true metagovernance review.

On the positive side, in the case of issue domains that are ready for negotiation, it is clear that the shift of focus from short-term cost cutting to the streamlining of the governance regime (with a view to permanently reducing costs in the medium and longer run) is bound to free the evaluation process of some of its least desirable fixtures. Such a shift is also likely to make some progress possible in issue domains, where some preliminary work on the governance front would appear to be absolutely necessary before one can proceed to any meaningful form of negotiation. Furthermore, in these kinds of issue domains, it seems probable that attempts at proceeding before having built the required bridging capital may not only be entirely useless, but also quite toxic.

Broadening the perspectives to take into account a longer time horizon and a broader systemic view (issue domain rather than program) modifies the evaluation necessary to arrive at wise decisions with the whole system – something that is crucial for the governance of issue domains comprised of self-organized networks that must be nudged along (catalyzing the underpinning social learning), rather than through edicts.

The shift from instrumental to ecological rationality imparts a revolutionary twist to the evaluation process. This broader perspective contributes to freeing the approach from myopia, tunnel vision, and the tyranny of what Edmund Husserl called "misguided rationalism."[222] This shift – from a perspective on policy that is mired in target-shooting fantasies (that grossly overestimate our agency in dealing with always evolving, ill-structured problems) toward a perspective that emphasizes intelligence, innovation and experimentalism – should allow policy to escape from unhelpful strictures.

Finally, the governance perspective forces attention on the need to emphasize the process of organizational redesign that is necessary if a more effective, efficient and economical mode is to be found. This is done not by focusing exclusively on process, but by focusing on the way to intervene subtly, to ensure that the self-organized network will improve its learning abilities and attenuate its learning disabilities through efforts to make it more 'delayered,' participative and sensitive to local circumstances.[223] This seemingly indirect and roundabout way of proceeding, far from being ineffective, is likely to generate more substantial and sustainable financial savings in the longer run.

However, dealing with issue domains in parallel without imposing a simplistic cost-cutting template will not necessarily be easy. The cumulative impact of myopia, tunnel-vision and instrumental rationality (together with the presumption that the Jacobine State is the sole avenue for the emergence of any meaningful expression of the public interest) has generated a phenomenal dynamic conservatism.[224] This means that, even though we know that our present ways are ineffective, the emotional cost of scrapping much of our unhelpful accumulated intellectual capital is very high.

---

[222] Gilles Paquet. 2009. *Crippling Epistemologies and Governance Failures*. Ottawa: University of Ottawa Press, chapter 1.

[223] Gilles Paquet. 2008. *Gouvernance: mode d'emploi*. Montreal: Liber.

[224] Donald A. Schön. 1971. *Beyond the Stable State*. New York: Norton.

There is still an immense resistance to accepting the challenges of small 'g' governance. Governance is fundamentally subversive. It reveals the pathologies of existing governing arrangements that have been built on corporatist interests, and that do not serve the citizenry well. Only the pending crisis in the governing of healthcare may bring our democracies to their senses. For, as the OECD reminded Canada recently, the current ways of governing our healthcare regime can only lead to its implosion.

Conclusions

The case for a true metagovernance review is strong, and the powers of dynamic conservatism and ineptitude are not infinite. Our two illustrations have shown the merit of tackling issue domains in the way we suggest. The fact that there also seems to be no readily available alternative approach that appears to be technically feasible, socially acceptable, implementable, and not too politically destabilizing – and that there is no hope that these problems will simply fix themselves – would appear to strengthen the case for a true metagovernance review.

Our cases show that a more participative and focused approach to issue domains is likely to generate reforms at the governance level that promise more than short-term financial savings. The roundabout nature of this approach does not ignore the need to be more cost effective and cost containing, but it suggests that these objectives may be secured more intelligently by taking a longer term perspective.

The major hurdles to action on this front are not ignorance about what needs to be done, but mental 'prisons' that prevent action from being taken.

| Appendix

Statement of understanding and mutual respect

K ahnawake and Québec, recognizing the importance of cooperative endeavours and wishing to maintain a constructive relationship on the basis of their respective principles and concepts found in the Two Row Wampum and in Government Policies on Aboriginal matters and in particular in the National Assembly Resolution of March 20th, 1985, reaffirm their commitment to the Statement of Understanding and Mutual Respect which they have signed on the 15th day of October 1998. They therefore renew their agreement to the following declaration of reciprocal political commitment.

Kahnawake and Québec, as represented by the undersigned, favor the route of discussion and negotiation for concluding and signing agreements that will be negotiated in various fields of jurisdiction.

With a strong sense of their respective culture, language, custom, laws and traditions, Kahnawake and Québec agree to negotiate with mutual respect for their national identities and each other's history and territorial occupation.

Kahnawake and Québec further agree to participate as partners in various Kahnawake economic development ventures. Québec also agrees to develop financial and fiscal arrangements that would provide for Kahnawake's long term economic stability.

To accelerate the negotiation process and bring it to a rapid conclusion, Québec and Kahnawake each have already appointed negotiators and concluded a framework agreement with a view to the rapid conclusion of sectoral agreements in the various fields of mutual interest.

To insure continued understanding and mutual respect, Kahnawake and Québec recognize the importance of regular communications between their respective representatives, including at the highest level, and commit to meet on a regular basis and whenever necessary.

Nothing in this declaration prevents Kahnawake from continuing to exercise its prerogatives to conclude agreements with any other government, in the application of its jurisdiction through its legal institutions, and in accordance with its priorities.

Signed on the ____10____ day of ____June____ 2009.

_____
Michael Ahrihrhon Delisle Jr.
Grand Chief
Mohawk Council of Kahnawake

_____
Jean Charest
Premier Ministre
Gouvernement du Québec

_____
Pierre Corbeil
Ministre responsable
des Affaires autochtones
Gouvernement du Québec

Déclaration de compréhension et de respect mutuel

Conscients de l'importance d'une coopération active, les Mohawks de Kahnawake et le Québec, désirant maintenir entre eux une relation constructive basée sur leurs principes et concepts respectifs contenus dans la doctrine du Two Row Wampum et dans les orientations du gouvernement concernant les affaires autochtones et notamment dans la résolution adoptée par l'Assemblée nationale le 20 mars 1985, renouvellent leur adhésion à la Déclaration de compréhension et de respect mutuel qu'ils ont signée le 15 octobre 1998. En conséquence, ils réitèrent leur accord à la déclaration suivante d'engagement politique réciproque.

Les Mohawks de Kahnawake et le Québec par leurs représentants soussignés, privilégient la discussion et la négociation pour les conduire à la conclusion et à la signature d'ententes négociées dans différents domaines d'intérêt commun.

Fiers de leur culture, de leur langue, de leurs coutumes, règles et traditions, les Mohawks de Kahnawake et le Québec entendent négocier dans le respect mutuel de leur identité nationale de même que de leur histoire et de leur occupation du territoire.

Les Mohawks de Kahnawake et le Québec désirent également participer à titre de partenaires dans des projets de développement économique à Kahnawake. De plus, le Québec accepte de mettre en place des arrangements financiers et fiscaux propres à contribuer à la stabilité économique à long terme de Kahnawake.

Afin d'accélérer le processus de négociation et le faire aboutir rapidement, le Québec et Kahnawake ont déjà nommé des négociateurs et signé une entente-cadre en vue de la conclusion rapide d'ententes sectorielles dans les différents domaines d'intérêt commun.

Afin d'assurer le maintien sur une base continue de la compréhension et du respect mutuel, le Québec et Kahnawake reconnaissent l'importance de communications régulières entre leurs représentants respectifs, y inclut au plus haut niveau, et s'engagent à se rencontrer régulièrement et à chaque fois que le besoin s'en fera sentir.

Rien dans la présente déclaration n'empêche les Mohawks de Kahnawake de continuer à pouvoir conclure des ententes avec tout autre gouvernement, suivant ses propres priorités, dans l'exercice de ses compétences et par l'entremise de ses institutions légales.

Signée le _____10e_____ jour de _____juin_____ 2009.

Michael Ahrihrhon Delisle Jr.
Grand Chef
Conseil mohawk de Kahnawake

Jean Charest
Premier Ministre
Gouvernement du Québec

Pierre Corbeil
Ministre responsable
des Affaires autochtones
Gouvernement du Québec

| Conclusion

"The best way to predict the future is to create it"
— *Peter Drucker*

What has been proposed in this short book is not a template to be applied to the analysis of governing in all ways of life, but an approach to the subject of collaborative decentred metagovernance that is based on a recognition of the true weight of complexity and diversity, and their implications for human organizations and social systems. Such complexity and diversity have annoyed observers by introducing unwanted degrees of uncertainty, and led them to invent unduly crude representations of the systems to be governed that have erased or elided these crucial features. As a result, the chromatic and skewed images they have proposed of how governance plays out in reality have been most unhelpful as descriptions, and most deleterious as instruments to elicit effective governing arrangements.

The new collaborative decentred metagovernance approach that we have proposed heretofore is based on more realistic stylizations that give complexity and diversity their full measure and importance. These stylizations have built on the centrality of process, design and reflexivity, emphasized the importance of information, networks and collaboration in understanding the texture of organizations, and exorcised the arrogant and deterministic 'leadership' twist that has inflicted the notion that 'someone is always in charge' of the process of governing, and replaced it with a more realistic 'stewardship' twist that recognizes the contingency basis of the process of governing, and the immense role played by self-organization.

The first victim of the emergence of the collaborative decentred metagovernance approach is Big 'G' governing. It has slowly begun to be replaced by a small 'g' governance cosmology that is built around stewardship practices, rooted in inquiring systems and social learning. This introduced a much needed complexification of the stylization of the governing process – defined as the joint work of stakeholders in designing an environment of continuous maintenance and improvement, of the sort amenable to an automatic pilot capable of promising resilience and innovation – in the private, public and social sectors.

The second victim of the emerging collaborative metagovernance approach has been the mechanical and deterministic definition of strategy and policy in all sectors: this outgrowth of a goals-and-controls mindset has progressively begun to be replaced with a symbiotic conversation among stakeholders and with the situation, capable of eliciting the best possible tailored outcomes, but with the full realization that what will emerge, given the power of self-organization, may not be what was planned.

The third victim is the so-called collaborative state – a mischievous oxymoron – proposed by public administration experts to 'rescue' the failed old public policy model by arguing that Big 'G' government might still reach its goals (always presumed to be the only legitimate expression of public interest) by 'engaging' with the citizenry. They suggest that Big 'G' + citizen engagement somehow equals collaborative decentred metagovernance, while, in reality, it is nothing of the sort. It is not even a version of 'collaboration lite,' but an attempt to defend the Big 'G' government cosmology, and to hollow out the notion of collaboration which is at the core of the co-production of governance.[225]

---

[225] Simon Parker and Niamh Gallagher, (eds). 2007. *The Collaborative State*. London, UK: Demos; Don Lenihan. 2011-2012. "Rescuing policy: The case for collaboration," *Policy Options*, 33(1): 42-45.

In a Canadian context, for those who can still remember, this sort of attempt at instrumentalizing collaboration echoes the disingenuous McCamus-Drouin exercise, conducted in the early 1990s on how to rekindle prosperity. The utter disingenuity of the process was exposed when it was demonstrated that the minutes of the regional consultation meetings had very little to do with the contents of the final report.

The power of denial

With those three dragons having been slaughtered – Big 'G', the goals-and-controls view of policy and strategy, and the disingenuous ploy of state-engineered engagement – it might have been hoped that we could now proceed to construct an alternative small 'g' governance apparatus, focused on 'wayfinding,' experimentation with inquiring systems, and true partnership to take the place of the old artillery. But this would presume that the death certificates of the dragons have been acknowledged. This is not, however, the case. Despite its obvious failures, the old cosmology still dominates the scene to a great extent.

The resilience of the old paradigm is ascribable to different sets of forces in the case of the three sectors (private, public, social), and more generally, with respect to the role of the state in nations like Canada.

In the first case, the denial stems from an inability/unwillingness to accept that what is required is a reframing away from the thinking that invented hierarchy with cascading goals, precise role definitions, and elaborate rules and procedures to solve the main problems of efficiency and scale that bedevilled the socio-economy at the turn of the 20th century. These are not the problems of the day. It has been recognized by the most astute observers of the management and governing scene.[226] Market forces are pressing the private sector to adapt to the new realities and imperatives of the unforgiving and volatile new environment by adopting a much more fluid approach based

[226] Gary Hamel. 2009. "Moon Shots for Management," *Harvard Business Review*, 87(2): 91-98.

on social learning. But, the technocracy in the private sector is still reluctant to abandon the old cosmology and to embrace the new one because of the deadweight impact of the old paradigms in good currency over the last 50 years in which they have invested so much.

In the public and social sectors, the adjustment has been even more successfully opposed by the bureaucrats because of the absence of market pressures, and also because of the sacralization of their work and their old ways as, by definition, a response to a higher calling than the travails of the less worthy and less reliable private sector. These ill-founded beliefs have become not only a protective belt for the old cosmology, but also nothing less than ideological mental prisons tending to immunize the traditional paradigm from any critical questioning. Public and social bureaucrats have come to define themselves as a new selfless and enlightened clergy, whose ways could not be questioned since they are agents of the public interest. Without a counterweight to this disinformation and propaganda, these views have crystallized and become a sort of commonplace conventional wisdom, making it not only difficult, but almost dangerous to challenge them, because of the toxic imperative of political correctness.

This overwhelming *pouvoir social* (as Tocqueville would have called it) has discouraged critical thinking and stunted social learning.[227] As a result, (1) the state is still regarded as the only credible rampart against governance failures, despite its ongoing record of doing nothing of the kind; and (2) the state has lionized the powers of hierarchical goal-

[227] Raymond Boudon. 2005. *Tocqueville aujourd'hui*. Paris: Odile Jacob, 168ff. The toxic impact of *le pouvoir social* is extremely important in a large number of areas: it explains the mental prisons in healthcare (where even though other systems making use of user fees and private sector hospitals are performing much better than the Canadian system based on state monopoly, these instruments remain taboo) or in dealing with our catastrophic productivity performance (because productivity has been transmogrified into a Bay Street concern, and not one linked with the general level of welfare).

and-control policy and strategy making and has blinded the citizenry to the possibilities of what they can do together: inquiring systems, experimentation, efforts to nudge existing organizations, etc.

No need for undue pessimism

What has fundamentally prevented a more effective questioning of the old ways is the dual handicap of:

1. the lack of a clearly defined alternative to the traditional Big 'G' government-way that can be defined in operational and practical terms in all sectors, and the difficulties and complexities of the alternative language of problem formulation; and

2. the new responsibilities and the new burden of office of key stakeholders in a metagovernance world, that has led them to shy away from adopting an approach that imposes heavier demands on them.

It is our hope that collaborative decentred metagovernance can provide a sufficiently clear alternative approach that may require a new slightly more complex vocabulary than the traditional one, but that promises to generate a much less superficial understanding of the world of governing. The fact that it may require some intellectual investment, more critical thinking, and more accountabilities and responsibilities for stakeholders, may be a hurdle. But the accumulation of evidence of the failure of the traditional ways in all sectors is bound to erode the cognitive dissonance somewhat, and to make stakeholders less reluctant to embrace a new approach that promises a greater capacity to nudge organizations and social systems in preferred directions.

A not insignificant factor that may tip the balance toward being more willing to reframe perspectives to be able to reconfigure organizations more effectively is the advantage of facing a complex, diverse, fractious and turbulent environment – in a state akin to *surfusion* – the slightest impact at some well chosen pressure points may

trigger abrupt dramatic transformations.[228] The challenge is
to identify the relevant blockages, and the loci of potential
tipping points.

The road to transformation might be usefully
characterized as being best addressed in three separate but
complementary ways:

1. **the demolition of myths and ideological barriers**
   that prevent stakeholders from gaining access to a
   comprehensive view of the world (i.e., one that does not
   suffer from as much false consciousness). This calls for
   hard hitting attacks on these mental prisons, and stark
   confrontation with those spreading the falsehoods;

2. **the production of a broad framework or cosmology**
   capable of providing a fairer and less inadequate
   approximation of the field of inquiry. This requires the
   development of a refurbished frame of reference that
   organizes the objects of the inquiry in a manner that is
   heuristically more powerful; and

3. **the design of inquiring systems and experimentations**
   capable of bringing forth the sort of automatic-pilot-type
   governing system likely to generate the appropriate mix
   of resilience and innovation. This demands creativity,
   but also a very clever use of the context and the forces of
   self-organization.

[228] Hubert Reeves has illustrated this physical phenomenon by telling the
story of the some 1,000 horses forced by a forest fire to jump in Ladoga
Lake in the winter of 1942 to save their lives. Even though the temperature
had been very cold over the last few days, the lake was still liquid. But
while the horses were swimming toward the other side of the lake, the
lake suddenly froze. The day after, the horses were found transformed
into ice monuments at the centre of the lake. Reeves explains that the drop
in temperature over the last days had been too rapid: the water did not
have time to freeze and remained liquid at a temperature below zero. But
the water was unstable, and a slight shock could trigger an instantaneous
crystallization into ice (Hubert Reeves. 1986. *L'art de s'enivrer*. Paris: Seuil).
Hervé Sérieyx has applied this concept to organizations and shown how
unstable organizations and social systems could crystallize into a new
form as a result of small impacts at tipping points (Hervé Sérieyx. 1993. *Le
Big Bang des organizations*. Paris: Calmann-Lévy).

Much progress has been accomplished on all these fronts over the last while. On the first front, Big 'G' government, shared values, 'leadership', etc., have been challenged frontally; on the second front, the notions of collaborative governance, stewardship and the like have been developed; and on the third front, experiments with various mechanisms and instrumentations have been carried out by Elinor Ostrom and her team, by Charles Sabel, and by many others using a variety of tools that have proved very effective in different contexts.

What is necessary now for the reader to realize is that professional competence in governance, as in other professions, comes with practice, and with the sort of connoisseurship that can only be developed and honed in action. One does not learn the skills required to be a neurosurgeon, French horn player, or hockey player in a textbook. The textbook prepares the candidate for action, but it is from action and practice that competence flows.

Developmental evaluation as a point of entry

It is not always clear where to start in such a quest. But our experience suggests that it is often easier to modify the technology than the structures, and easier to modify the structures than to confront the basic idea of what the organization or social system is about.

As Donald Schön reminds us, any organization or social system is made up of a theory (defining what business it is in), a structure (roles and responsibilities of stakeholders) and a technology (tools and techniques, both hard and soft).[229] These components are interdependent, and one cannot change without inducing change in the others. Very often, a change in the technology is easier to effect, and carries with it changes in structure and theory. For instance, the traditional scoreboard in accounting (financial statements centred on rates of return of the capital invested by shareholders) considerably limits the accounting vista. It occludes the role of many other key stakeholders, and cripples any analysis one might build on

[229] Donald A. Schön. 1971. *Beyond the Stable State*. New York: Norton, p. 33-37.

146 | STEWARDSHIP

such reductive accounts. Refurbished accounting scoreboards (for instance, shifting to one based on the analysis of the surplus generated, and the way it has been distributed among stakeholders)[230] opens the way to a much more sophisticated X-ray of the operations of a firm, and the door to the sort of negotiation at the core of collaborative decentred metagovernance.

The same may be said about governance in general. A good way to open a discussion about collaborative decentred metagovernance may be to start with the sort of traditional data gathering and assessment method in use, and then to show in what ways they are reductive and not that helpful in providing the necessary guidance for resilience and innovation. But it may also open the door to deeper forms of collaboration.[231]

The sort of evaluation in good currency in the old paradigm is, broadly speaking, an *ex post* autopsy of the performance of the organization that is exclusively centered on certain indicators suggested by the goal-and-control approach. As a result, such an evaluation, focused on narrow marksmanship, is reductive and distortive, since it focuses only on certain dimensions of the operations to the exclusion of much that is essential to the life of organizations and social systems.[232]

Reflecting on a new and better way to undertake evaluation – a crucial portion of the process of social learning – is a most effective way to probe:

- what is useful and sensible for evaluation of a complex adaptive system;
- the focus on contextually sensitive situational adaptations and development;
- not being satisfied with improvement on what is but development outside the box;

[230] Jacques Perrin. 1977. "Comptes de surplus. Pour un nouveau tableau de bord de l'entreprise," *Revue française de gestion*, n° 11, p. 35-40; Gilles Paquet. 2008. *Gouvernance : mode d'emploi*. Montreal: Liber, chapter 3.
[231] Gilles Paquet. 2005. *The New Geo-Governance – A Baroque Approach*. Ottawa: University of Ottawa Press.
[232] Michael Quinn Patton. 2011. *Developmental Evaluation*. New York: The Guilford Press.

- sustaining relationships being more crucial than meeting targets;
- not being limited to exploitation of resources but aiming at innovation;
- the (considerable) dependence on social learning for exploitation and exploration;
- learning loops at many levels that need to be monitored; and
- the importance of *bricolage* and redesign as levers.

In response to the perceived incompleteness of traditional evaluation, developmental evaluation has recently emerged.

> [It] centers on situational sensitivity, responsiveness and adaptation... tracks and attempts to make sense of what emerges under conditions of complexity, documenting and interpreting the dynamics, interactions, and interdependencies that occur as innovations unfold... including changing the evaluation design, reconfiguring program theory, and responding to emergent stakeholder needs... supports learning to inform action that makes a difference... involves questioning the assumptions, policies, practices, values, and system dynamics that led to the problem in the first place and intervening in ways that involve the modification of underlying system relationships and functioning.[233]

Thus, it forces a review of the existing structures and even of the theory underpinning the organization.

Developmental evaluation would appear to be ideally suited to the collaborative decentred metagovernance approach. The governing apparatus or automatic pilot of a complex adaptive system is an inquiring system focused on the 'development' of the organization or the social system through social learning in context.

So both the developmental evaluation and the governing apparatus will have to transform, depending on contexts, and on the phase in Figure 7 in the organizational ecocycle, discussed in chapter 4, for instance. The transitions between the phases may be impaired by different traps (rigidity

---

[233] Michael Quinn Patton, 2011, p. 7-11.

between 2 and 3, mental blockages between 3 and 4, lack of resources between 3 and 4). This entails a continuous re-jigging of developmental evaluation, depending on the phase in the ecocycle under consideration.[234]

The requisite variety and collaboration imperatives

This short book was not meant to comprehensively review all that a new toolbox might contain. Rather, it was meant to generate some interest in the use of the collaborative decentred metagovernance approach.

This endeavour raises two challenges.

The first challenge is meeting the constraint of Ashby's law of requisite variety, which states that one cannot regulate a system of a given level of complexity without using an instrument of at least the same degree of complexity.

So in the face of complex adaptive systems, governing requires an assembly of a variety of mechanisms in the 'automatic pilot' to match the complexity of the evolving organization and context, for, in each set of circumstances and fields, the inquiring system would aim to operationalize this approach and to clarify the sort of protocol to be used at each of these stages. We have not been too prescriptive here by intent – for issue domains vary greatly, and require processes adjusted to their idiosyncrasies. As the previous case studies have shown, it would appear that the collaborative decentred metagovernance approach cannot avoid tackling this challenge of designing the optimal mix of mechanisms of coordination (i.e., making it as simple as it can be but as complex as it needs to be).

The second challenge is the collaborative imperative. This work of coordination cannot be done without explicit effort to mobilize the information, knowledge and skills available across the members and the groups. This commands the design of social learning mechanisms that facilitate and foster

[234] Michael Quinn Patton, 2011, chapter 7.

collaboration. Indeed, nothing less than a 'deepening' and 'widening' of the collaborative process is required.[235]

The 'deepening' of true collaboration has been explored thoroughly. It demands much more than information sharing or a forum; it calls for synchronized behaviour – relationships with other persons that will modify their behaviour to synchronize it with yours. This entails fostering group identity, and collective decisions and a commitment to provide a particular effort together. Collaboration is not simply informing and educating the other, or gathering information, and it goes beyond discussing and engaging somewhat. It connotes true partnering.[236]

As for the 'widening' of the collaborative process, it connotes the possibility of mobilizing mass collaboration by tapping into the immense reservoir of cognitive potential available in the population in general.[237] This is based not only on the human propensity to cooperate, but on the highest and best use of self-organization and mass collaboration, as reported in the works of Tapscott and Williams, and Elinor Ostrom, for instance.[238]

In praise of humility

It is the compounding of complexity and diversity that will force social scientists to ultimately abandon their antiquated

---

[235] Gilles Paquet. 2011. *Tableau d'avancement II – Essais exploratoires sur la gouvernance d'un certain Canada français*. Ottawa: Invenire, chapter 13.

[236] The Health Canada Policy Toolkit for Public Involvement in Decision Making (2000) has an illustration of the densification of relations to connote this deepening, but it is not sufficient. Collaboration entails a degree of commitment that echoes a certain *affection societatis* – a commitment to creativity, imagination, and gumption in support of the partnership. In French law, failure to live up to such a commitment results in an abrogation of the partnership.

[237] Clay Shirky. 2010. *Cognitive Surplus – Creativity and Generosity in a Connected Age*. New York: The Penguin Press.

[238] Don Tapscott and Anthony D. Williams. 2006. *Wikinomics – How Mass Collaboration Changes Everything*. New York: Portfolio; Elinor Ostrom. 2005. *Understanding Institutional Diversity*. Princeton, NJ: Princeton University Press.

approaches and adopt collaborative decentred metagovernance as a more promising strategy of governance.[239] Indeed, the volumes in this series will illustrate how inquiring systems are the only way to recast the policy process, if there is any hope of eliciting the sort of automatic pilot required to achieve the hoped for resilience and innovation.

This is not a regime for the timid: the task is daunting and the probability of success is not necessarily high, at least not in the short run. But this approach is bound to throw much light on the process of governance, and to lead to a great deal more social learning. By failing better and by learning from it, we might be able to do much better in the long run.

In a quantum world, there can be no assurance of certainty that governance will succeed. The best we can hope for is success through failure.[240] In fact, the success that can be achieved through social learning will undoubtedly be ascribable, to a major extent, to effective 'fail-safe' and 'safe-fail' mechanisms succeeding in reducing harm.

In order for such an approach to be envisaged by key stakeholders in the private, public and social organizations however, it will be necessary for them to acquire an important virtue – humility – that will help them to understand that in the face of the most complex issues of the day, they must accept that they may not know what to do, and will need to experiment over and over in order to acquire the knowledge they do not have. Only then will there be a willingness to bet on inquiring systems, social learning and experimentation.

From our experience, there are signs that such humility might be emerging.[241]

[239] Scott E. Page. 2011. *Diversity and Complexity.* Princeton, NJ: Princeton University Press.

[240] Henry Petroski. 2006. *Success through Failure – The Paradox of Design.* Princeton, NJ: Princeton University Press.

[241] Dan Gardner. 2012. "The Power of Political Humility," *Ottawa Citizen,* January 4, www.ottawacitizen.com/technology/power + political + humility/5942771/story.html?id=5942771.

| References

Some segments of this book have been previously published in a somewhat different form.

R. Hubbard and G. Paquet. 2011. "The Case for a Fundamental Governance Review" in C. Stoney and G.B. Doern (eds.). *How Ottawa Spends 2011-12*. Montreal: McGill-Queen's University Press, p. 60-83.

G. Paquet and C. Wilson. 2011. "Collaborative Co-Governance as Inquiring Systems," *www.optimumonline.ca*, 41(2): 1-12.

R. Hubbard and G. Paquet. 2012. "Public Policy as Inquiring System: The Case of Health Care" in G.B. Doern and C. Stoney, (eds.), *How Ottawa Spends 2012-13*. Montreal: McGill-Queen's University Press, (in press).

Titles in the Collaborative Decentred Metagovernance Series

Other titles published by INVENIRE